T0283176

"There are so many things to wonder and worry about as it relates to our children. *How to Help Your Child Clean Up Their Mental Mess* gives the tools to ensure amazing mental health for your child. You may end up correcting some of your mental mess too!"

Michelle Williams, speaker, author, and singer

"Dr. Leaf's newest book is an essential guide for anyone who wants to teach their children how to improve their cognitive functioning, emotional resilience, and mental strength. When we teach our kids to master their minds, we teach them how to become the master of their lives, and this book will show you how to do this!"

Jim Kwik, leading brain coach and *New York Times* bestselling author of *Limitless*

"Dr. Leaf's Neurocycle offers a revolutionary five-step approach to navigating big feelings—and it's as helpful for the parent as it is for the child."

Melissa Urban, *New York Times* bestselling author of *The Book of Boundaries*

"These days, it's a must to raise emotionally strong and resilient kids. This book is a must-read for anyone who wants to help children navigate mental health struggles and give them the tools to deal with the ups and downs of life without feeling defeated."

Jordan Harbinger, creator of *The Jordan Harbinger Show*

"Dr. Leaf demonstrates deep empathy and compassion alongside an excellent grasp of the scientific significance of what we know about the developing brain. This excellent resource should be essential reading not only for parents but for all professionals tasked with helping children to grow healthily in what can, at times, be a toxic and challenging culture to survive."

Dr. Sami Timimi, visiting professor of child psychiatry at the University of Lincoln, UK, and author

"In this book, Dr. Leaf proposes simple, accessible, evidence-based mental health strategies you can teach children to help them process life events and deal with mental health struggles. The advice in this book will help children to better navigate the challenges of growing up."

Dr. Joanna Moncrieff, psychiatrist, author, and professor at University College London

"Dr. Leaf has again synthesized for us a wealth of wisdom and experience to produce a 'scientific, evidence-based first step in dealing with the crisis in children's mental health through mind-management.' She does this through building a thorough foundation and instills hope by offering parents simply profound tools for daily use, which will help instill better and better self-regulation in our children, allowing them to grow and mature in natural, God-given ways."

Robert P. Turner, MD, MSCR, QEEGD, BCN, associate professor of clinical pediatrics, Medical University of South Carolina

"Dr. Caroline Leaf's new book is a timely and critically important guide for families everywhere to keep marching forward toward the inner peace, emotional and mental well-being, and fulfilling life we all want. The intense silent suffering at the hands of our own thoughts can be overcome once and for all with the powerful, practical tools Dr. Leaf so aptly lays out. What better gift to give your family and children than the gift of peace?"

Kimberly Snyder, *New York Times* bestselling author of *You Are More Than You Think You Are*

"There are two things the education system fails to teach us: how to truly operate and thrive in our body, and how to truly operate and thrive in our mind. And this book is that recipe for teaching our children how to thrive in their minds and bodies. This should be an essential part of our global education system."

Vishen Lakhiani, founder and CEO of Mindvalley and bestselling author

"As parents, this topic is close to our hearts. It is comforting to receive a message of hope and to be shown how we can help our children learn to manage their mental health. Dr. Leaf gives parents and guardians a science-based system to help them teach their kids to go through the challenges of life and define their own unique story. We strongly recommend this book."

Colleen and Jason Wachob, cofounders and co-CEOs of mindbodygreen

"I love the practical advice in this book and wish I'd had it when my own three kids were younger. It's a must-read if your kids are managing anxiety, depression, bullying, or really any mental health struggle. Dr. Leaf gives you real-life strategies so you can help your children not only deal with whatever life throws at them but feel successful in everything they do."

Mel Robbins, *New York Times* bestselling author and award-winning podcast host

"Dr. Leaf has a wealth of knowledge that is useful for parents and children. This is an excellent guide to help kids learn how to not let the challenges they face stop them from living their best lives and achieving their dreams."

Nedra Glover Tawwab, LCSW, therapist, *New York Times* bestselling author, and relationship expert

"These days, our ability to remain resilient and fully functional in the face of the ever-increasing challenges of our world is threatened like never before. Gratefully, Dr. Leaf gifts us important tools to regain our composure and remain centered as we encounter life's obstacles. This is a book that will help so many."

David Perlmutter, MD, FACN, #1 *New York Times* bestselling author

"What if we could do more to foster resilience and good mental health from a young age? Dr. Leaf answers that question with science-backed research and tips for raising mentally strong children who are capable of managing and processing their emotions. Instead of repeating the cycle, we can help facilitate the change for the next generation."

Dr. Will Cole, leading functional medicine expert and *New York Times* bestselling author of *Intuitive Fasting* and *Gut Feelings*

"Wow, what a brilliant support for all parents of today. I love how Dr. Leaf uses science and personality to make the best mind-management tools so simple to use!"

Poppy Jamie, bestselling author, founder of Happy Not Perfect, and host of *Not Perfect Podcast*

"A must-read for any parent or guardian who wants to prepare their child to succeed in this world emotionally, mentally, and physically. This book will help you give your child the tools they need to manage mental challenges and live their best life!"

Ed Mylett, global entrepreneur, bestselling author, and top podcast host

HOW TO HELP YOUR CHILD

YOUR CHILD

Clean Up Their Mental Mess

HOW TO HELP YOUR CHILD

Clean Up Their Mental Mess

A Guide to Building Resilience
and Managing Mental Health

DR. CAROLINE LEAF

BakerBooks
a division of Baker Publishing Group
Grand Rapids, Michigan

Published by Baker Books
a division of Baker Publishing Group
Grand Rapids, Michigan
www.bakerbooks.com

Printed in the United States of America

Library of Congress Cataloging-in-Publication Data
Names: Leaf, Caroline, 1963– author.
Title: How to help your child clean up their mental mess : a guide to building resilience
and managing mental health / Dr. Caroline Leaf.
Description: Grand Rapids, Michigan : Baker Books, [2023] | Includes bibliographical
references.
Identifiers: LCCN 2022044042 | ISBN 9780801093418 (cloth) | ISBN 9781540900388
(paperback) | ISBN 9781493423408 (ebook) | ISBN 9781540903525 (audiobook)
Subjects: LCSH: Cognition in children. | Mind and body in children. | Positive
psychology. | Child mental health.
Classification: LCC BF723.C5 L426 2023 | DDC 155.4/13—dc23/eng/20221116
LC record available at https://lccn.loc.gov/2022044042

This publication is intended to provide helpful and informative material on the subjects
addressed. Readers should consult their personal health professionals before adopting any
of the suggestions in this book or drawing inferences from it. The author and publisher
expressly disclaim responsibility for any adverse effects arising from the use or application
of the information contained in this book.

Some names and identifying details have been changed to protect the privacy of individuals.

Brain-ee is a registered trademark of Dr. Caroline Leaf.

Brain-ee illustrations by Saraia Driver.

Baker Publishing Group publications use paper produced from sustainable forestry practices
and post-consumer waste whenever possible.

23 24 25 26 27 28 29   7 6 5 4 3 2 1

This book is dedicated to my exceptional family:
my husband, Mac;
my four children, Jessica, Dominique, Jeffrey, and Alexy;
and my two sons-in-law, Eli and Jay.

Every bit of research I do, every word I write, is guided by the depth of wisdom I gain from my relationships with each of you. The love we share is a love that lasts longer than time itself.

This book is also dedicated to every parent and every child. I want to let you know it's okay to be a mess, because we will clean up the mess together.

■■■■■■■

We don't have a mental health crisis; we have a mind-management crisis. It is the time and the season to honor the beautiful minds of our children and their individual stories.

■■■■■■■

Contents

Contents

Preface

Every day, it feels like we read another news report about the mental health crisis among children and youth, as well as how depression, anxiety, and suicide rates are getting worse.[1] Recently, the U.S. Surgeon General went so far as to issue an advisory to protect the mental health of youth.[2] Things seem bad, and for many young people, they truly are.

Although mental health challenges aren't new, they're different for each generation. Take bullying—it isn't a new phenomenon exclusive to the twenty-first century. Now, however, children take bullying home with them on their phone, tablet, or computer. No place seems safe. A great expanse of human social interactions has changed with the advent of the technological revolution. These changes have transformed the way many people, including children, perceive themselves and the world around them, which has contributed to increased feelings of loneliness and isolation among all age groups as we spend more and more time online and alone.

The world is changing, and sometimes it can feel like we're barely keeping our heads above water, whether we are parents, guardians, or vulnerable children just trying to figure out our place in the world. These feelings have been exacerbated through the recent pandemic and other major world events, which often make everything seem worse, further straining our sense of mental wholeness.

When it comes to addressing these issues, we must first acknowledge that we are more than just individuals with individual problems. We are humans in a community, which means we need to address mental health on both the individual and the communal level. According to the Mental State of the World Project, countries that score higher in individualism and performance orientation tend to have lower mental well-being metrics, while countries that score higher in group and family collectivism tend to have better mental well-being.[3] We cannot think of the child as only an individual; we have to consider the child in addition to the environment they occupy, including how we as adults manage our mental health and how this can impact our children.

Although mental health challenges aren't new, they're different for each generation.

We need to look at how we're teaching our children to process and navigate the new world in which we live. Are children being shown how to manage their mind? Are we teaching our children to navigate the highs and lows of life? Are we helping them understand, from youth, that where the mind goes, the brain and life follow?

This process starts with us as parents: how we manage our mental health is a model for how our children will manage their mental health. Research reflects that the unmanaged stress of an adult becomes the unmanaged stress of the child. So, one of the best ways you can help your child with their mental health is by working on your own mental health.

By implementing the methods in this book, you will learn how to successfully navigate the mental distress that comes from the messiness of life, and, at the same time, demonstrate to your child that it is possible to find peace amid the storms.

Our mind drives who we are: how we think, feel, and choose. Our mind drives how we wake up in the morning and start the day; how we show up throughout the day; how we interact with our family, friends, teachers, and environment; and how we manage the good and bad things that happen to us. Our mind drives how our body makes cells, impacting our biological health and how we absorb nutrition from our food.[4] The mind controls everything to do with our "aliveness." We can go for three weeks without food, three days without water, and three minutes without oxygen, but we don't even go for three seconds without using our mind!

If the mind is the driving force of our "aliveness" as human beings, we should be putting a massive amount of energy into understanding and developing the skills of mind-management to help both ourselves and our children manage the vagaries of life. A child with underdeveloped mind-management tends to be more vulnerable to intense feelings of confusion and be overwhelmed as they attempt to process what they're exposed to, because they don't have the mental skills necessary to understand what is happening to them or to communicate what they are going through.[5] It's our job as parents, caretakers, and educators to help them navigate a world that can easily feel scary and overwhelming. One of the best ways we can do this is by giving them the gift of mind-management.

■ ■ ■

In this book, I offer a scientific, evidence-based first step in dealing with the crisis in children's mental health through mind-management. I will give you easy-to-use, simple ways you can start teaching your child how to manage their mind so that as they grow, they can live their best life. Additionally, along the way you may learn a thing or two about how to manage your mind so that you, too, can live a life of resilience, peace, and joy.

The key to this book is understanding how the mind functions. I talk about how whatever we think about the most grows, how the brain merges with our environment, and how the mind drives this process. I also discuss in simple ways how you can communicate easily with your child, how an unmanaged mind can create a messy mind, and how this changes the brain through neuroplasticity, which contributes to feelings of fear, confusion, sadness, and being overwhelmed.

The story doesn't end here! The mind and brain can always change through directed mind-management. I have spent nearly four decades investigating how minds and brains work and have developed a simple, evidence-based system called the Neurocycle, which I discuss in this book. The Neurocycle works by identifying toxic thoughts and destabilizing them over cycles of 63 days by building up positive, healthy, reconceptualized thoughts. In this book, I teach you how to use this system with your child and give you steps, exercises, and practical examples to help you teach your child how to expand beyond mindfulness to embrace, process, and reconceptualize their experiences.

The mind and brain can always change through directed mind-management.

As you work through the information in this book, you will learn how to create a safe environment for your child to work on their mental well-being. You will learn how to give them the skills they need to be able to tell their own stories. You won't learn how to solve all their problems or make their pain go away, because this is impossible. You will, however, learn how to help them ask the kind of questions they need to and receive the kind of mental help they require.

When we help our children become more self-regulated in every way, including how they manage their emotions, behaviors, and perspectives, we teach them how to tune in to the messages coming from their mind, brain, and body and to use these to their advantage. As we do this, we create a space for our children to discuss and process what they see and hear both online and in real life. We help them get comfortable with facing the uncomfortable and teach them how to embrace their emotions and receive the messages those feelings bring them instead of being afraid of feeling sad or confused. In this way, we avoid pathologizing childhood and help them embrace their humanity.

In part 1 of this book, you will learn how to help your child understand the keys of how the mind functions. Part 2 shows you how to teach your child the Neurocycle for mind-management. In part 3, you will learn how to apply the Neurocycle in different situations, such as day-to-day struggles, trauma, sleep issues, and more.

To help you on this journey, I want to introduce you to Brain-ee!

Brain-ee is a cartoon character I developed that walks this mental health journey alongside your child, which will help make talking about their mental struggles easier. Brain-ee is used throughout the book to explain the concepts in a visual way and is a great tool to help your child understand their emotions and what they are going through. You can even get Brain-ee as a toy for your child at drleaf.com to help comfort them and teach them how to communicate when something is wrong and when they need help.

PART 1

THE KEYS TO UNDERSTANDING HOW THE MIND FUNCTIONS

In the following chapters, I help you understand—and help you help your child understand—the mind-brain-body connection, what thoughts and memories are, and the importance of self-regulation.

1

■■■■■■■■

The Mind-Brain-Body Connection

> Whatever we experience with our mind goes through the brain
> and the body, which is why mind-management is so important. If
> we don't manage the impact of our experiences, they can affect our
> mental *and* physical well-being.

In this chapter, I introduce how the mind-brain-body connection
works so that you can have a better conceptualization of how to
help your child understand the way their thoughts can impact
how they feel mentally and physically.

The thing we need to remember is that children are often a
lot more insightful than we give them credit for. However, since
they're still growing and developing, they often don't know what
to do with everything they observe and experience. It's easy for
children to feel overwhelmed by the vast expanse of information
absorbed through the mind and brain daily.

With or without mind-management, just by virtue of being
human, children wire life experiences into the neural networks
of their brain and throughout their body *with* their mind. This
process changes the mind, brain, and body—it has an impact,

which will manifest itself in how a child functions mentally and physically. We are psychoneurobiological creatures, and the mind, brain, and body are intricately connected.

For example, say your child is anxious. The "thing" that's making your child anxious is an actual physical thought made of stimulus responses inside memories in their brain.[1] The mind comprises the action of them worrying or being anxious about this thought. The more your child worries about this thought, the more it can impact them on both an emotional and a physical level (the body), including physical illness symptoms such as an upset stomach or heart palpitations.[2]

If your child has ever had a tantrum, I'm sure you know how this feels. If they are worried about school, for example, and get very upset when you try to get them ready in the morning, this is a warning signal that's emerging from their thoughts, which, in turn, were built into the brain by their mind based on the way they processed their experiences.

To better understand this, think of a garden. When the garden is messy and full of weeds, it does not look or feel good. When a mind is like a messy garden, it feels like it's not working, and things quickly seem to spiral out of control. On the other hand, when the garden is blossoming and healthy, a few weeds or a storm may have an impact but do not affect the long-term health of the garden.

Thankfully, there are great systems in the mind, brain, and body that can help us teach our children to build a healthy garden in their mind. When they learn how to manage their mind, they can make the mind-brain-body connection work for them, which will help them deal with the impact their experiences have on them, no matter their age.

This begins by observing the signals sent by the mind, brain, and body. These signals can be categorized into four main components, emotions, behaviors, bodily sensations, and perspectives,[3] which I discuss in detail in chapter 3. A big part of mind-management is tuning in to these signals to find the story they're attached to and then changing how this story plays out inside of us *and* in our future. This involves self-regulation, which helps us to stand back, observe ourselves, and monitor how we interact with the world.

Understanding the Mind

Understanding this process of mind-management begins with understanding the mind. The mind is how we think, feel, and choose in response to everything going on around us while we are awake. The mind's thinking, feeling, and choosing work together as a team to "grab" our life experiences and put them into our brain as energy.

This energy results in structural changes in the brain that contain the memories of our experiences, which cluster together into a thought like the branches on a tree. These changes are driven by the mind through a process known as neuroplasticity.[4] The mind essentially plants our experiences into the brain as "thought trees."[5] Thought trees are the neurons made of axons and dendrites in the brain.

Here are two images to help you understand this. The first is a drawing of axons and dendrites on a neuron. The whole neuron is the thought tree, and the dendrites are the memories in the thought tree.

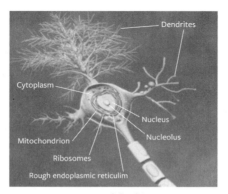

Axons and dendrites

This next image is what these thought trees look like inside the brain.

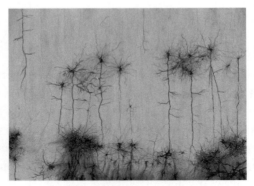

A collection of "thought trees" or neurons

The mind uses the brain to store what it experiences—that is, the events and circumstances of life—as "thought trees." We respond and react to these experiences while we're awake and sort them out while we sleep, which is why we have dreams and nightmares.[6] A thought is therefore the product of the mind-in-action. A thought is a physical thing made of proteins and chemicals that occupies mental real estate in the brain as a tree-like structure of our neurons *and* as gravitational fields in the mind *as well as* in the cells in our body.

This is why the brain is often described as a neuroplastic responder. Each time it's stimulated by our mind, it responds in many ways, including neurochemical, genetic, and electromagnetic changes. This, in turn, grows and changes structures in the brain, building or wiring in new physical thoughts. The brain is never the same because it changes with every experience we have, every moment of every day, and when the brain changes, the body changes as well.

The mind builds all these daily life experiences into our brain and body and fixes them at night when we're asleep. The mind is therefore more than a machine that runs nonstop. It's an incredibly complex driving force that runs the brain and the body. The mind "shows up" in the brain and the body and becomes our sentience. Our mind is where our identity and uniqueness are formed. It is where who we are is recognized—our consciousness.

In terms of the mind-brain-body connection, the brain and the body are the physical parts made of matter, whereas the mind is the energy part made of electromagnetic waves and gravitational fields.[7] They're separate but inseparable, because they all need to work together to function as a living human in the world. This means that whatever we experience with our mind goes through the brain and the body, which is why mind-management is so important. If we don't manage the impact of our experiences, they can affect our mental *and* physical well-being.

The mind itself has three parts, the biggest of which is the nonconscious mind. The nonconscious mind is massive and never goes to sleep. It's extremely intelligent, is incredibly fast, and can work on multiple things at once to keep us alive and functioning. It monitors all our existing thoughts and the memories they are made of, and it's always looking for whatever is worrying or affecting us in some way to help us repair it and restore balance.

When the nonconscious mind finds a thought that is worrying us, it sends it up through the second part of the mind, the subconscious mind, which is like a bridge between the nonconscious mind and the conscious mind. According to my theory, called The Geodesic Information Processing Theory, the nonconscious mind operates 24/7 and is what drives us. It feeds information into the conscious mind that then shows up in our "symbolic output," which comprises what we feel, say, and do, how we feel in our bodies, and our perspectives.[8]

Unlike the nonconscious mind, which works 24/7, the third part of the mind, the conscious mind, is awake only when the body is awake and is much slower than the nonconscious mind. The nonconscious mind processes about 90–95 percent of everything we are exposed to at any given moment, but the conscious mind is able to focus on and process only about 5–10 percent.[9]

As mentioned above, one of the main jobs of the nonconscious mind is to scan all the information in the neural networks, root out the toxic stuff, and make us consciously aware of it. This is where the conscious mind is really good at stepping in and grabbing these toxic thoughts from the nonconscious mind, deconstructing them, and reconstructing them so they don't affect our mental and physical health. The more we learn to manage our mind through self-regulation, the more we activate this dynamic interplay between the conscious and the nonconscious mind—our built-in protective mental health system![10]

The Neurocycle

The scientific system of mind-management I have researched and developed, the Neurocycle, forms the basis of this book. It will help your child develop communication between the different parts of their mind and learn how their mind affects their brain and body. It will teach your child how to understand the messages from their nonconscious mind and prevent toxic thoughts and memories from getting stronger and affecting their mental health.

When we learn to manage our mind and change our perceptions, as I observed in my most recent clinical research study, we can change our brain's response, our physiology, and our cellular health, which play back into our mind because of the feedback loop between the brain and the body.[11]

Mind-management is one of the most effective ways to build up a child's resilience because it teaches them to focus less on what happened to them and more on what they can do about it. It helps children contextualize their life experiences instead of just diagnosing them and giving them a label based on a vague set of symptoms. It goes beyond the current system of biological mental health care to address the whole child: their biology, their community, their psychology, their individuality, and their story.

Our life is the product of our experiences, which becomes our individual life story. When we give children the mental tools to meet their needs, we give them the tools to tell their own stories. We can teach them that although we can't always change what happens to us, we can change how it impacts us and plays out in our life.

Your Child's Innate Resilience

This involves actively learning how to see things from our children's perspective. They are the experts on who they are and the lived experiences they have, and it's our responsibility as the adults in their life to validate their uniqueness, support them, and help them embrace, process, and reconceptualize their own narratives.

Indeed, given that perils and strains in life are natural, unavoidable, and inevitable, parents, caretakers, and teachers have a responsibility to help children develop their innate resilience—to teach them to grow and learn from diverse life experiences. Yes, we need to protect our children as they grow into adults, but we also need to give them the tools to manage failure and painful experiences, because these are an inevitable part of life.

I would go as far as to say that protecting our children means teaching them how to manage life even when we are no longer there to safeguard them. If we immerse our children in messages that failures and hurtful experiences will do lasting and irreparable damage to them, we will negatively affect their ability to develop resilience. As Greg Lukianoff and Jonathan Haidt note in their book *The Coddling of the American Mind*, we have developed a "modern obsession with protecting young people from 'feeling unsafe'" that, in many ways, is inhibiting their ability to feel able to meet life's challenges. This is possibly "one of the (several) causes of the rapid rise in rates of adolescent depression, anxiety, and suicide" that we observe in our world today.[12]

Similarly, in his book *Antifragile*, Nassim Nicholas Taleb discusses the concept of *antifragility* as a way of understanding resilience.[13] In the same way that our immune system builds defenses against disease by the *presence* of disease in the body, humans need the presence of challenges to repair, learn, adapt, and grow. Without challenges, our natural, inbuilt antifragility (or resilience) can become inflexible, fragile, and inept. We aren't helping our children's mental health when we try to protect them from everything bad that can happen. Given that risks and stressors are natural parts of life, we should help our children develop their innate capacity to grow and learn from their life experiences.

We aren't helping our children's mental health when we try to protect them from everything bad that can happen.

Fortunately, we live in an era where it is increasingly common to speak about mental health issues. More and more people are aware that it is normal for children and adults to struggle mentally and that we all need help at times. This has opened the conversation and turned something that has often been hidden and misunderstood into something that can be understood and managed.

Every day, we are learning more and more about how we function as human beings and how, when it comes to the mind-brain-body connection, there is always hope. Regardless of how young or old we are, we have an immense capacity to change.

2

■■■■■■■

What Are Thoughts?

The good news is that you can make ugly thought trees into healthy, strong trees just by using your mind!

In this chapter, I explain what a thought is in simple terms that you can use to help your child understand. The explanations below are written to help you explain these concepts in simple and meaningful ways, but you can adapt the language according to your child's needs and learning level. I recommend reading through this chapter several times and making some notes for yourself before explaining what a thought is to your child.

Brain-ee wondering what thoughts are

What Are Thought Trees?

For Your Child

Everything you experience becomes a memory inside your brain. When you play with your friends, when you watch TV, when you listen to your teacher—all of this goes into your brain as memories. These memories join together into big thoughts, which look like trees. These trees are your special stories—no one else has "thought trees" like yours!

We all have lots of stories because there is always a lot going on every day. This means that we have many thought trees growing in our brain, which is like a big forest. Many are happy thought trees, like playing with your friends at school, but

Brain-ee thinking

some thought trees are sad, like a time when you hurt yourself while riding your bike or a time when someone said something mean to you and made you cry.

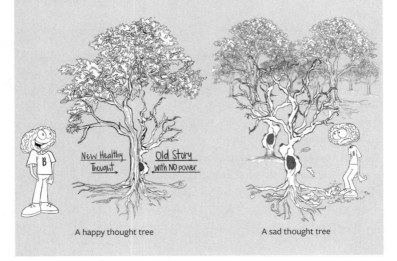

New Healthy Thought → Old Story with NO power

A happy thought tree   A sad thought tree

Roots, Trunks, and Branches

To help your child understand the concepts in this section, you could help them grow a plant from a seed. You could do this in a jar, garden, or window box and make this an interactive mental health experience. The explanation below is aimed at ages 6 and up. For ages 3–5, just use the happy and sad thought trees and explain how these form in their head because of what has happened to them and that, together, you are going to make the sad trees into happy trees.

How thought trees grow over time

For Your Child

Trees come from seeds planted in the ground. First the roots grow, then the trunk, and then the branches. "Thought trees" grow in the same way: first the roots, then the trunk, and then the branches. The roots of the thought tree are the detailed memories of what your story is, and they hold the thought tree in the brain. The trunk is how your mind, brain, and body are trying to make sense of your story. The branches of the thought tree are how you understand your story and how you respond to the story. The branches are how people see you and how you see yourself through this story.

Everything we feel, say, and do comes from our thought trees. For example, our emotions, like being sad or happy, come from our thought trees. So do all the words we speak and the things we do, such as playing, drawing, watching movies, running, fighting, and so on. In fact, we can't do, feel, or say anything without thought trees!

In the same way that a tree needs food and water to grow, the thought trees in our head also need food and water to grow. The difference is that the water and food for your thought trees are your thinking, feeling, and choosing—your mind.

These trees are really cool! They help you feel, say, and do things. They tell your tongue to move to make the words that come out of your mouth, and they tell your body to move to do things like riding a bike. For example, when you learn something new at school, like your ABCs or how to multiply in math, this new information will grow into your brain as a thought tree as your teacher explains how to do it. Then, when you practice your ABCs or math equations, the tree grows stronger! In fact, as you continue practicing your ABCs or math, you grow more roots and branches, and the tree gets bigger and stronger and looks nice and healthy.

Thought trees also grow in our head when something bad happens, like getting teased at school. This can make us feel sad, and we might feel bad about ourselves. This type of thought tree does not look so pretty, but the good news is that you can make these ugly trees healthy!

I want to introduce you to Brain-ee, who will help you learn how to make the sad thought trees healthy. Brain-ee is your friend and will help you understand why you feel unhappy or angry as well as how to make things better. Actually, I am going to tell you a secret: Brain-ee is a superhero who is going to teach you his special superpower called the Neurocycle, which will help you find and fix the messy thought trees that are making you feel bad.

When you do the Neurocycle, you are being a real superhero!

Superhero Brain-ee

A child's negative experiences will always be with them, so it is important to clarify that we cannot "erase" the bad thoughts as though they never happened. Rather, through the Neurocycle, we are helping them to manage negative thoughts and experiences. Our goal is to reconceptualize what happened to them so that they don't feel they are defined by their bad experiences.

Brain-ee strolling happily through
a forest of thought trees

3

What Are Warning Signals?

> Warning signals are messengers that tell us that something is going on in our life. There is always a "because" behind how your child is showing up, and their warning signals point toward this "because."

Warning signals are messengers that tell us that something is going on in our life. There is always a "because" behind how your child is behaving, and their warning signals point toward this "because." These signals are attached to the thought tree that is impacting their mental well-being.

If we pay attention to these warning signals, this awareness pulls the thought tree they are associated with into the conscious mind. As we do this, we will see more information about these signals in the branches of the thought tree (see the image below). As soon as this happens, the thought tree changes and becomes weaker so you can help your child work on managing and changing it.

There are four warning signal branches. One branch represents the *emotional* warning signals, or what your child is feeling, such as sadness, happiness, anger, and so on. The next branch represents

their *behavioral* warning signals, or what they are saying and doing. The following branch represents
how they feel in their body, which comprises
the *bodily sensations* they experience. The
fourth branch represents what they are
thinking about themselves and how they
are looking at their life in light of what
has happened to them; these are the
perspective warning signals.

These four warning signals are
messengers. They tell you something
about your child's mental health. By
teaching your child to pay attention to
these signals, you will help them tune
in to these four signals and begin the
journey of working out what they are
pointing to and what this means for their
mental health.

Brain-ee gathering the
warning signal branches

It takes time to unpack these signals and to work on the thought
behind them, though sometimes this can happen quickly. Other
times it takes a bit longer, depending on whether the issue is a big
trauma, a small trauma, or just a day-to-day issue.

As you help your child unpack these signals, you will teach
them how to begin finding the origin story in the roots of a particular thought tree. Getting to the roots allows them to begin the
process of reconceptualizing the experience in a way that works
for them rather than against them. This means they will still have
this thought tree as part of their story (or part of their forest of
thought trees), but they will see it in a way that is more manageable for them. The key here is to teach your child how to manage
the hard parts of life so they are not completely overwhelmed or
beaten down by the challenges they face.

This may seem complicated, but it gets easier with practice and
is incredibly empowering. For example, the new signals coming

from the reconceptualized thought can be "calm feelings" instead of "worry feelings" as your child begins to understand where the anxiety they were feeling was coming from and what to do about it. Through this process, they will not only better understand why they feel the way they do—both mentally and physically—but also gain more insight into their behaviors and perspectives.

Looking at the Four Warning Signals

The process of exploring warning signals is an intrinsic part of the Neurocycle, as I will discuss in part 2 of this book. It will teach your child that the way they see themselves and the world is affected by the experiences they have been through and that they can change their perspective through their thinking—they are not powerless. They will be empowered to recognize when they are in a state of mental distress and have a system in place to manage this distress.

I cannot emphasize enough how much a child needs to feel emotionally safe and validated when processing their reactions to life. This is why the Neurocycle is such a powerful mind-management tool. It isn't designed to simply swap one behavior for another. Rather, it's a science-based technique to help you and your child understand why your child is behaving in a particular way—as seen through the four signals—and how to manage it. So this goes beyond mere awareness. The Neurocycle gives your child the mental tools to find the *why* behind what they are demonstrating and how to change it.

The Neurocycle gives your child the mental tools to find the *why* behind what they are demonstrating and how to change it.

If your child is struggling with their mental health, the Neurocycle teaches them that it is happening not because of *who they are* but because of *something they have been through*. Instead of being confused or overwhelmed by their emotions, behaviors, bodily sensations, or perspectives, they will be encouraged to embrace these signals and to use them to change their mind. They will see the message in the messiness of life!

For Your Child

I have good news for you! If you don't like what you are feeling, doing, and saying or how your body feels, you can use your superpower, the Neurocycle, to find the thought tree that is making you unhappy and make it better and healthier, which will make you happier!

The first step to make this Neurocycle superpower work and find those unhappy thoughts is to look for something called your warning signals, which are the branches on a thought tree. First, look at the picture of the thought tree. These are the warning signals you need to find: how you are feeling, what you are saying and doing, what you feel in your body, and how you feel about life at this moment. The warning signals are telling you something is wrong. It's like they are shaking the leaves to get your attention, and when you pay attention to them, they pull the thought tree forward that they are attached to.

Below is a summary table of these four warning signals and examples of how you can explain these signals to children of differing ages.

TABLE 1

The Four Warning Signals

WARNING SIGNAL	QUESTIONS TO ASK WHEN DOING THE NEUROCYCLE	EXAMPLES	
Emotions	Ages 3–5: Are you sad, mad, etc.? Ages 6–10: What are you feeling?	• Sadness • Anger • Frustration • Irritation • Guilt	• Shame • Anxiety • Depression • Fear • Confusion

WARNING SIGNAL	QUESTIONS TO ASK WHEN DOING THE NEUROCYCLE	EXAMPLES
Behaviors	**Ages 3–5 (actions, behaviors, words):** I see you are doing X; why are you doing that? Are you doing X because of Y? **Ages 6–10:** What are you doing? What are you saying? How are you saying it?	• Speaking very fast or slow • Not speaking much • Using lots of emotional words • Throwing tantrums • Bed-wetting • Fighting with siblings/friends • Being lethargic • Shouting • Throwing things • Crying • Shouting and using angry words • Not wanting to play
Bodily Sensations	**Ages 3–5:** What is sore/"uncomfortable" in your body when you feel X? **Ages 6–10:** What are you feeling in your body? How does your body feel when you are sad, angry, or happy (such as having an upset tummy when you are worried your friend won't play with you)?	• Upset tummy • Sore head • Tongue stuck to palate • Tension in shoulder and neck muscles • Shivering
Perspectives*	**Ages 3–5:** You know how people use glasses to see? Well, sometimes your thoughts are like a pair of glasses, and they make you see the world in a different way, like if you were wearing different colored glasses. Do they make the world darker or lighter? Do things seem scary or not scary? **Ages 6–10:** How is what you are thinking making you see the world? How is what has happened making you look at your day? Does this make you feel more or less happy? More confused or less confused? What do you think about the world? What do you think about your life?	• Scared • Confused • Hypervigilant • Hypovigilant • Irritated • Angry • Depressed

* Note to parent: Perspective can be difficult to explain to your child and is often related to how they feel emotionally. This is an attitude, mindset, way of looking at something, or way of seeing the world and life over a specified period of time (be it a few minutes, hours, days, or even months). By acknowledging that your child has their own perspective, you are acknowledging them as a unique being with their own opinion on how they view the world based on what they have experienced.

The Four Warning Signals

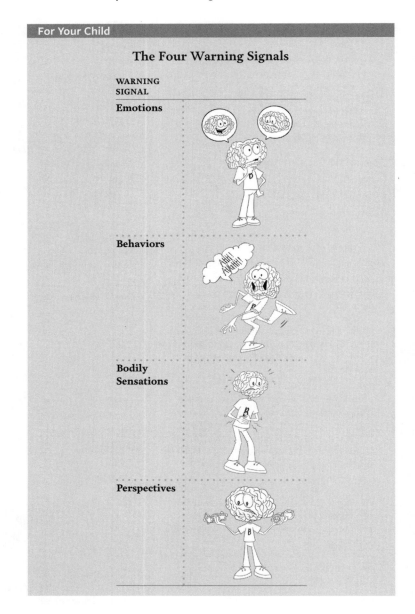

The Difference between Healthy and Unhealthy Thought Trees

Below is a way you can explain the difference between a healthy thought tree and an unhealthy thought tree to your child. You can adapt the language based on their level of understanding.

For Your Child

What does a thought tree look like in your head? If it's a sad or unhappy story, it's a messy tree. It may even have thorns on it, so when you remember the thought with all the memories, it makes you sore in your mind and body in the same way a thorn hurts you when you touch it.

On the other hand, if it's a happy story, it's a beautiful green tree. Being with people you love, doing things you like to do, and playing with your toys are all examples of experiences that can grow beautiful green trees in your head and make you feel good. Your mind tells your body about the happy or excited thought trees, and this can make you feel very good and want to jump up and down or laugh.

However, when people are mean to you, you have bad dreams that scare you, or bad things happen to you, you grow a messy tree, which will have messy branches (warning signals). You know how sometimes you get an upset tummy when someone teases you at school or when you are scared of your schoolwork? Well, this is because something happened that caused a messy thought tree to grow in your head. Then your tummy may hurt because your mind tells your brain and every part of your body about the messy thought tree, and that makes the body sad—your body tells you this through the pain you feel. This is not your fault, because the tree grew due to something that happened to you, but it can make you feel frightened or unhappy.

The bigger the story is and the longer the story has been going on, the larger the thought tree will be. For instance, if other children have been teasing you for a long time, the tree might be quite big and affect you in a bad way. But you can change these unhappy trees! You are very special because you can fix the messy trees and make them better if you don't like them. You get to decide what your own thought forest looks like in your head. If the thought trees are making you feel scared, angry, unhappy, or hurt, you can fix the trees. If it's a really bad thought tree, you can dig down to the roots and make them better so they grow into a strong, new, and beautiful green thought tree to make you feel better.

You can even build more branches on the beautiful thought trees that make you happy. These trees make your brain and body really healthy, and you will feel much stronger the more you water them with your mind. You can learn how to do all of this using Brain-ee's amazing superpower, the Neurocycle.

Brain-ee looking at a messy,
unhealthy thought tree and a
healthy, green thought tree

4

Superhero Brain-ee's Superpower: The Neurocycle

The Neurocycle is a systematic and deliberate process designed to help us direct the neuroplasticity of the brain. It essentially teaches us how to manage a messy mind and brain and, in doing so, to manage our mental health.

Introducing the Superpower: the Neurocycle

The Neurocycle is a systematic and deliberate process designed to help us direct the neuroplasticity of the brain. It essentially teaches us how to manage a messy mind and brain and, in doing so, to manage our mental health. The Neurocycle can be used to manage the day-to-day struggles of life and traumas as well as to grow new habits in the brain.

The Neurocycle system is based on thirty-plus years of research and clinical applications of the mind-brain-body connection, the science of thought—how thoughts form, what thoughts are, and how they drive how we function—and how we can influence all of this. For more on the science of the Neurocycle, see my book *Cleaning Up Your Mental Mess*.

Before going through the 5 Steps of the Neurocycle, it is important that you prepare your mind, brain, and body for the neuroplastic changes that the Neurocycle activates.

Brain Preparation

Brain preparation exercises are activities that help to settle down the neurochemical and electromagnetic waves in the brain and body. These decompression-type exercises are important, because when we experience toxic stress, the mind-brain-body connection quickly becomes chaotic, which makes it hard to think or act clearly. When we calm down the mind, brain, and body, we can start to get to the root of what is affecting us.

Brain-ee doing breathing exercises

Now, let's take a look at the 5 Steps.

The 5 Steps

The power of the Neurocycle lies in its simplicity. It's a five-step process that, when used correctly, makes profound changes in how the mind and brain work.

The 5 Steps are:

1. **Gather Awareness**: become aware of warning signals associated with a thought tree—that is, what you are feeling emotionally and physically, how you are behaving, and your perspective.
2. **Reflect**: reflect on *why* you feel the way you do.
3. **Write/Play/Draw**: organize your thinking and reflections to gain insight. For your child, this step will look different depending on age. The play and draw options are added for younger children.
4. **Recheck**: look for patterns in your life, your relationships, your responses, your attitudes, and so on.
5. **Active Reach**: take action to reinforce the new, reconceptualized pattern of thinking you want in your life (which replaces the old toxic cycle).

Essentially, the first three steps of the Neurocycle, **Gather Awareness**, **Reflect**, and **Write/Play/Draw**, systematically bring the thought into the conscious mind, which weakens the power the thought has had over your child. Then the **Recheck** step weakens this control even more through evaluation, which leads to the acceptance of the issue—*This has happened, and I can't change that*—and its impact in their life, followed by the redesigning aspect—*This is what I can do about it*. The **Active Reach** helps implement this newly redesigned/reconceptualized thought through practice and keeps your child from going back and getting stuck with the old thought through overthinking and ruminating. All of this collectively builds up your child's mental resilience.

Analogies for Your Child

Here is a simple way to introduce and talk about brain preparation with your child. You can refer to this often.

For Your Child

Sometimes our thought trees and their branches can feel out of control, like how a big storm in a forest makes everything swoosh around or sometimes even breaks branches in the wind or causes trees to catch fire from the lightning. It is normal for things to feel out of control sometimes, especially when something sad or horrible happens to us.

Thankfully, there are ways you can prevent the storm in your head from hurting you. You can build a shelter in your thought forest or use an umbrella to keep your mind safe from the storm. This is what breathing exercises or other calming activities do when you are in distress—they're like a shelter or an umbrella to keep you safe from the "emotions and other warning signals storm." You can't stay in that shelter or under that umbrella forever, but these exercises will give you a chance to wait for the storm to calm down so that you can start working on making the thought trees healthy.

The brain preparation exercises are like building a shelter or holding an umbrella in your thought forest—they will keep you safe from the storm

Now, here is a simple way to introduce and talk about the Neurocycle with your child. You can refer to this often.

We all have unhealthy thought trees in our mind, like this:

An unhealthy thought tree

However, we can use Brain-ee's superpower, the Neurocycle.

STEP 1: GATHER AWARENESS STEP 2: REFLECT STEP 3: WRITE STEP 4: RECHECK STEP 5: ACTIVE REACH

Brain-ee's superpower: the Neurocycle

When we do, we can grow healthy thought trees that look like this:

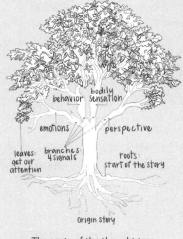

behavior bodily sensation
emotions perspective
leaves: get our attention branches: 4 signals roots: start of the story
Origin story

The parts of the thought tree

Remember the thought tree I spoke about earlier? The **roots** of the tree are the memories of the original experience—the story of what happened to you.

The **trunk** makes meaning out of the roots as it transforms the roots into the branches. The trunk determines what kind of branches grow from the roots. If the roots are sick and messy, the branches will be sick and messy too.

The **branches** of the thought tree give you information about how you see and understand what happened to you and/or how you see yourself. These are the four warning signals. Sometimes these trees are unhealthy and make us sad. So, we use your Neurocycle superpower to make this unhealthy thought tree better.

This how we do it: first, you need to **Gather Awareness** of how you are feeling by observing your warning signals (the branches of the thought tree) more deeply. This is kind of like observing and describing the "symptoms" of the thought tree. For example:

- "I feel worried and frustrated." (emotional warning signal)
- "I want to cry and not talk to anyone." (behavioral warning signal)
- "I have an upset tummy." (bodily sensation warning signal)
- "I hate school." (perspective warning signal)

The **Reflect** and **Write/Play/Draw** steps will help you understand the story that the symptoms are pointing to. You can ask yourself questions like:

- *Why do I feel worried and frustrated?*
- *Why do I want to cry and not talk to anyone?*
- *Why is my tummy upset?*
- *Why do I hate school?*

The **Recheck** step will help you work out how to fix this unhealthy tree and its messy roots—it is the mending that your tree needs to grow strong! In this step, you will use your Neurocycle superpower to explore your feelings and thoughts and try to find a way to make what happened to you better. For example, you may be sad or frustrated because you kept messing up your work and cried, your friends laughed at you, and your teacher shouted at you. You know it is okay to be sad, and this won't stop you from doing your work again because you know your mom will help you understand it at home so you can do better next time. You know that when you take your work to your teacher tomorrow and show your friends what you learned, you will show them that you can do the work and that it's okay to cry sometimes if something is hard. You know you aren't stupid because it's okay to make mistakes—that's how you will learn!

Your **Active Reach** is like taking "medicine" each day to help the thought tree get healthy. For example, you have decided to tell yourself seven times today, *I am not stupid, I am learning.*

5

■■■■■■■■

Helpful Guidelines

The key thing to remember as you work through the Neurocycle with your child is *flexibility*, especially with young children. Try not to be too regimented and try to be patient with yourself and your child. Remember, this whole system is designed and structured to help reduce stress, not increase stress.

The Developmental Table

The table below provides a simple overview of the developmental stages for the age ranges I cover in this book. You will see the age group on the left. On the right is a basic description of how children think, feel, and choose at this particular age, as well as typical social and language skills—which will also, of course, depend on the child in question. I also explain in a general way how to use the Neurocycle at each stage.

Developmental Stages and Details

AGES	DEVELOPMENTAL DESCRIPTION

3–4[1]

Mind (Thinking, Feeling, Choosing)

Children ages 3–4 generally recognize that their mind, body, and emotions are their own. They are beginning to understand the difference between basic emotions such as sad, happy, afraid, angry, and so on. Their nonconscious mind is developing at a faster rate than their conscious mind, which is why they understand more than they can actually express.[2]

Social Interaction

They are beginning to understand the concept of "mine and yours," are sharing more, and are becoming more imaginative. Imaginary friends are common at this age—your child can tell the difference between fantasy and reality but often uses fantasy to understand reality, which is because the nonconscious mind is developing so fast. They are becoming more independent, are generally very active, and respond well to enactment and game-style demonstrations. They can develop a fear of imaginary things, care more about how others act, and show affection for familiar people, so these are the kinds of things that shape their attitude(s). Ideas of empathy can be demonstrated to children using imagination, play, or real-life examples.

Language

They are increasingly curious about everything, including their body, and their language development is prolific. They generally will construct sentences of three to six words. They understand many of the things you say and, although it is very fragile, often have good insight into their own value and self-worth.

With This Age Group, Use:

Demonstration, enactment, and physical items. I suggest getting four shoeboxes and covering them nicely—let your child help you do this. Next, cut out pictures from magazines, coloring books, and so on that represent the four warning signals: emotions, behaviors, bodily sensations, and perspectives. It is important to have pictures of young children's faces as well as those of older children and adults. You or your child can also draw pictures or use objects and toys. This preparation can be done as an activity with your child. Children as young as 2–4 have a fairly insightful understanding of many emotional concepts, much more so than we used to understand. However, they don't yet have the linguistic cues to fully describe and explain what they feel. This is where we come in as adults and provide words and ways of expressing themselves using movement, enactment, toys, pictures, music, storybooks, and so on.

AGES	DEVELOPMENTAL DESCRIPTION

5–6[3]

Mind (Thinking, Feeling, Choosing)

This is the age when most children start school, so their intellectual abilities, social abilities, and play are starting to become more complex and will involve other people and personalities. During their pretend play, they may start expressing more complex ideas and emotions, as their mind is grasping the world around them on a deeper level. You might notice fewer outbursts as they develop better ways of understanding and even managing their emotions. They are also more likely to pick up on social cues and understand that constant outbursts may not always be beneficial to them. You might also find that your child has more patience and is more able to use their reasoning. They are also able to understand basic emotions and will most likely express them in a clearer way.

Social Interaction

During ages 5–6, family is still the most important communal point for a child, but they will start to develop more independence and make friends outside the family unit. They are also actively pursuing and adding to their relationship circle, which is when they are truly able to harness skills of empathy (although ideas of empathy can be demonstrated to children as young as 2). Children at these ages develop more complex play patterns and have more complex interactions with their peers. They may create more plots alone or together in their play or try to work together at a task. You may also find that your own interactions with them change as they are better able to understand their emotions and the conversations you share with them.

Language

They will, most likely, start talking a lot more and express more ideas using language. They will likely talk a lot to themselves, and their conversations will be complex as they listen to and observe many of the adults around them.

With This Age Group, Use:

Play, toys, and art. These will help your child understand more complex emotions. They can practice using these objects or play to express more complex feelings during the different stages of the Neurocycle. You can have your child draw or interact with the 5 Steps and engage in complex conversations about the meaning of emotions and thoughts. You can even incorporate different types of arts and crafts, such as LEGOs or other more complex children's toys, while walking them through the Neurocycle. They may even want to direct this process more once they get the hang of it.

AGES	DEVELOPMENTAL DESCRIPTION

7–8[4]   **Mind (Thinking, Feeling, Choosing)**

Children ages 7–8 tend to show more independence and start to think about the future and their place in the world. They are most likely beginning to understand how they view themselves and the world around them—their unique belief system is clearer, although it will be highly based on what their parents or closest relatives believe. They are more likely to be able to distinguish between fantasy and reality, which means they are also more likely to understand logic, emotion, and reason. They also tend to be very aware of the need to find a solution to a certain emotion or problem they are facing.

Social Interaction

Being accepted by friends is very important at this age. Children generally want to start taking responsibility for little tasks and talk more about school, friends, movies, games, books, and so on. They are also more likely to understand and infer that actions have emotions attached to them and that people often communicate through emotions. This is a great time to reinforce empathy and teach your child that there are deeper meanings behind our physical displays of emotions. Children at this age are generally able to understand that other people see and experience the world differently and can use that to interact with another person on a deeper level or interpret how the person is communicating or acting.

Language

They have a better grasp of language and are therefore better able to express themselves and talk about their thoughts and feelings. They are also becoming more aware of other people's feelings and can communicate this more. They also have generally developed their reading skills and comprehension, so exposing them to many books—written for this age group—that are related to emotions is very helpful and will teach them how to look for connections in the world around them.

With This Age Group, Use:

Social interaction. Generally, at this age, they want you to get involved. They respond very well to Neurocycling because it appeals to their increasing curiosity about the world around them as well as their developing logic. They can help you cut out pictures that show the four warning signals and can help you write examples of each of them on little strips of paper to put in each warning signal box. They will be able to do a lot more writing than children ages 5–6, so work with them as much as possible.

You may also find that conversation topics may include more serious emotions or things your child is exposed to. At this age, children are able to understand things like violence, hurt, peer pressure, and sexuality. They may have many questions, and it is important to be open and honest with your child—all these topics can be talked about without giving explicit detail. This is also a good age to introduce symbols or metaphors to your child as you work through or talk about different emotions or actions.

AGES	DEVELOPMENTAL DESCRIPTION

9–10⁵ **Mind (Thinking, Feeling, Choosing)**

This is generally when your child is entering the preteen stage. A number of children may experience puberty at this age, which will dramatically change the way they feel and experience the world.

Indeed, whether they reach puberty or not, at this age your child will be experiencing much more complex emotions. They will question rules more as they understand more, which isn't always a bad thing; they are using their ability to think deeply to see and examine inconsistencies and things that may not always make sense to them.

At this age, many children become more aware of their body and more familiar with how it looks and feels, and they will start forming a "body image" and a sense of their perceived place in the world. During this time, it is incredibly important to help your child form a more positive body image through encouragement and acceptance of all body types.

Social Interaction

Peer pressure really begins to impact children in this stage of life as they look to their social world to determine how they want to act, talk, think, and so on. Their friendships will be more complex, and they will bond on a much deeper emotional level with people they make friends with. As they do this, they will develop their empathy skills and dive deeper into what it means to interact with other people and understand that others' experiences are different from their own. This is a great time to teach your child to try to understand where other people are coming from.

Language

They will generally be able to have longer and more complex conversations and will understand more things, even if they don't always use a sophisticated vocabulary to express what they know. They tend to understand more symbolism in language and are better able to grasp belief systems and worldviews. They may also be able to have longer conversations about justice, the rules of society, and other more complex topics.

With This Age Group, Use:

Techniques that encourage autonomy and empowerment. After a few rounds of the Neurocycle, your child may develop a sense of how to lead the process while you facilitate. However, I do want to emphasize the importance of honoring your child's privacy at this point in their life. There may be things they want to write down and work through without you observing or helping them, and that is okay. Creating an open environment where your child can express opposing views by engaging in discussion will also allow your child to be more open with you.

Try establishing a "no judgment zone" when you help them work through the steps of the Neurocycle or when they go through them on their own. In this zone, your child can say or write down almost anything as they work through their emotions and understandings of life. This will help them develop their sense of autonomy by allowing themselves to feel their emotions, followed by analyzing and breaking them down, and then focusing on conscious ways of figuring out how to move forward. You may find that you will learn a lot from engaging in these types of conversations with your child! This is also a great way to create a space to normalize emotions that seem "crazy."

During this process, try to use activities that focus on your child's interests. They may have very specific interests by this age, such as sports, movies, books, hobbies, and so on. This is also the age when more specific feelings of anxiety or depression tend to occur. You will begin to see a lot more "grown-up" emotions in your child. Addressing these by encouraging your child to explore their emotions and their solutions is important in helping them create lifelong self-regulation habits.

The Three Keys of Neurocycle Communication

Working through the Neurocycle with your child is a wonderful opportunity not only to help them develop their mind-management skills and learn how to improve their mental health but also to connect with your child on a deeper level, which is one of the most important things you can do.

The Neurocycle system, by its nature, draws on three specific types of interaction that engender trust between parent and child, laying the groundwork for a beautiful and long-lasting relationship. I call these overarching types of interaction the three keys of Neurocycle communication.

Key 1: Allow yourself to respond to your child's struggles without judgment of who they are as a person. This is a good way to make your child feel heard and emphasize their value as a unique human being. For example, it might seem like your child has a bad attitude toward you, but in reality they are just irritated about something specific. So, instead of reacting and saying, "You have such a bad attitude!" you can describe what you see. "I see you seem irritated. Is there a reason why?" Your child will feel heard when you respond in this way rather than judged and dismissed. Further, because they feel heard, they will listen to and interact with you on a deeper level. This occurs throughout the Neurocycle, particularly in the Gather Awareness step.

Key 2: Show you care about what your child wants and needs. In the midst of the busyness of life, it's easy to approach your child with demands and instructions, telling them what they need to do. Of course, things do need to "get done" in life, so I'm not saying this desire is wrong. However, you need to make sure you ask your child what they need and want as well. This will validate what your child needs and show them how much you value them.

Key 3: Encourage your child to give their perspective and viewpoint without shutting them down. You are listening with the purpose of understanding what they are thinking about. This lays the foundation for a collaborative and facilitative relationship that builds and strengthens your child's reasoning and deep, intuitive thinking skills as well as empathy.

6

■ ■ ■ ■ ■ ■ ■ ■

The Power of Self-Regulation

Self-regulation is the single most powerful skill we can teach our kids because it is a surefire way to build sustainable resilience for life.

Doing the 5 Steps of the Neurocycle develops our self-regulation, which is a critical skill that helps us maintain and improve our mental health. Self-regulation is managing how we use our mind. As mentioned in chapter 1, our mind is how we think, feel, and choose, and self-regulation is how we *manage* this thinking, feeling, and choosing. We do this by examining and managing the four warning signals discussed in chapter 3.

The image below is of Brain-ee feeling really bad looking at his four warning signals and asking, *How am I feeling? What am I doing and saying? How does my body feel? What is my attitude? Why am I showing up this way?*

Brain-ee wondering, "Why am I showing up this way?"

We can learn to self-regulate our thinking, feeling, and choosing while we are awake. This isn't self-preoccupation or just taking an inventory of our feelings. Rather, self-regulation is a deliberate and intentional choice to stand back and observe the way we are showing up and adjusting this as needed. It's not mindful awareness alone. It is mindful awareness *and* going beyond that to do something with what we are now aware of. This can occur either in the moment or over time to help us deal with established patterns that have become disruptive habits.

The Neurocycle will help your child develop self-regulation skills. This mind-management process gives them a tool to deal with their thought trees. It is designed to help them face and deal with their struggles.

In fact, the organized self-regulation of the Neurocycle cultivates and activates the natural resilience we have as humans, helping it grow stronger over time. Resilience is a process and is linked to flexibility, or what I call the "possibilities mindset." It's characterized by feelings of *I will do what I must do to get this done. I will get through this. This happened; now what can I do about it?* This kind of mindset will help your child adapt to future crises, challenges, and emotional outbreaks. It is intrinsically hopeful and empowering.

This is important because we can often get stuck in our thinking when we believe something must be or go a certain way. A possibilities mindset essentially recognizes that there is always more than one way to go about things. We don't have to get stuck when something doesn't go a certain way or work out as planned. There are multiple possibilities we can choose from as we go through our life and focus on our goals. Allowing for different possibilities will prevent us from feeling defeated when we fail.

Initially, you will be co-regulating alongside your child as they learn to understand and use the Neurocycle. Co-regulating is a comfortable and perceptive interchange between the parent and child that provides facilitative support, collaborative coaching, and modeling to help the child observe, understand, and manage their thoughts and the subsequent emotions, behaviors, bodily sensations, and perspectives attached to them. As their ability to self-regulate develops, your co-regulation role will change. You won't stop helping them but rather will move from a leading role to a facilitating role.[1]

As your child works through the Neurocycle, they will recognize that the struggles they're going through are very real and that you acknowledge and validate their distress. They will see that they are not alone, that it's okay to ask for help, and that they can work through what they are facing and learn how to cope with and manage their pain.

Unfortunately, many adults have told me that they never learned how to interpret what they went through as a child, so they suppressed their mental pain, which eventually unraveled in their life and made their mental health worse. This isn't surprising, as suppressed and undealt with issues and trauma make us vulnerable to all sorts of mental and physical problems. The pressure builds like a volcano and explodes, negatively impacting what we think about ourselves and what we say and do—our warning signals. In many ways, our unhealthier reactions to life are a means of coping in the moment, a way of protecting ourselves from emotions we don't understand. However, these feelings and behaviors are not sustainable in the long run and often make things worse if they are not managed.

Thankfully, using the mind-management skills in this book, you can be proactive and give your child the gift of self-regulation. You can teach them from when they are young so that they learn how to manage the many ups and downs life will throw their way regardless of their age.

One great way to tell your child about the Neurocycle is to liken it to walking through a forest full of thought trees. Using imagery or toys here is a great way to explain this to young kids.

Brain-ee walking through a forest of thought trees

You can explain to your child that, like Brain-ee in this picture, they have their own personal forest in their mind that they need to take care of like a gardener. When they have a sad or unhappy tree that looks a little messy, they can take care of it and make it healthy and strong, just like getting rid of weeds or watering a tree. Making sure it has enough nutrients makes it stronger.

For example, your child might have gotten into a fight with a sibling and may feel very upset. They may struggle to let go of the fight, and a few days later, they get into another fight and bring up the past fight—they are clearly still offended by what happened. Essentially, this situation is affecting how your child is behaving. In this instance, you can explain to your child that the memory of the first fight is a growing thought tree in their head, which impacts how they feel and how they are acting toward their sibling. This thought tree is messy and thorny, and its leaves are wilted. However, because they are a "mind gardener," they can use the Neurocycle to fix this tree.

It is important to explain to your child that this process doesn't mean getting rid of the sad tree or destroying it. They are not trying to forget their experiences or get rid of them. In fact, we can't do this because our stories never go away; we just change them. Your child is learning how to see the tree in a different light or redesign it in such a way that they can learn how to live with it— it is no longer messing up the thought tree forest in their head.

As you can see in the comic strip below, in the first image Brain-ee is trying to get rid of the thought tree, but his story won't go away, so he only manages to expose the roots that are rotten. In the second image, Brain-ee is clearing away the dirt so he can put plant food on the rotten roots to mend them. In the third image, Brain-ee is replanting the mended roots so the tree can regrow in a healthy way. In the fourth image, the tree is almost better at 21 days. Last, in the fifth image, it's all better at day 63!

To redesign the tree, we need to look at the roots. As mentioned earlier, the roots are the memory of the origin story or experience

What happens when Brain-ee goes through the 5 Steps of the Neurocycle

that planted the thought tree. You can explain to your child that they must dig around the thought tree and examine the roots to see what is causing the tree to look so messy and unhealthy.

As your child goes through the Neurocycle steps, they are essentially "mending" the messy roots. If they do this over 63 days (the minimum amount of time it takes to build a new thought or memory; see chapter 12), the tree will regrow and become healthy. Multiple cycles of 63 days may be needed depending on how toxic and established the roots have become. However, as the picture to the right shows, over time, the memory of the old tree— the experience—will still be there, but it will be smaller and won't have the same power as the healthy tree. This is what it means to reconceptualize an experience. We are not

New Healthy Thought

Old Story with NO power

Brain-ee feeling much better because now he has power over the old story trying to teach our children to forget or erase what happened to them; we are teaching them to find ways of managing the messiness of life.

Some thoughts and their associated emotions will take more time than others to work through, because some experiences have a larger impact on how we think, feel, and choose. This is normal. The important thing is to let your child know that it's okay for them to feel sad and experience other emotions. As mentioned above, when you let your child know that they don't have to ignore or suppress these feelings, you help them understand that it's like a winter forest in their mind—they won't feel like this forever, and springtime will come again soon.

Brain-ee feeling much better
after doing the Neurocycle

PART 2

HOW TO USE THE NEUROCYCLE WITH YOUR CHILD

In the following chapters, you will learn how to use the Neurocycle for yourself and how to teach and use it with your child to help them manage their mental health. Remember: it's you *and* your child's superpower to mental health freedom!

7

■ ■ ■ ■ ■ ■ ■ ■

How to Do Brain Preparation

When we calm down the mind, brain, and body, we can start to get to the root of what is affecting us.

Think about it like this: we all generally have first aid kits in our homes so that when anyone in the family gets a cut or a scrape, there will be ways to attend to that immediate wound. We are thus ready to tend to our immediate physical health problems, but we often don't consider that our mental health also needs tending. Here is an idea of something you can do with your child: sit down and create your own "mental first aid kit." Fill this kit with all the things that will help you and your child manage their mental health in the immediate moment of feeling overwhelmed. Keep this kit near your regular first aid kit to remind you that your mental health is just as important to take care of as your physical health. You could include a drawing that makes your child happy, for example, or maybe an object that calms them or temporarily distracts them such as a fidget spinner or a cute stress ball. You could even put in a photo of them at their favorite place or with one of their favorite people, a toy they love, or a book that calms them down.

Here are some simple brain preparation exercises you can do with your child before or after the Neurocycle process, or whenever needed.

Brain-ee doing breathing exercises

1. **Breath Work**

   A simple and generally foolproof decompression exercise for children ages 3–10 is deep breathing. One of the best ways to do this with your child is by teaching them to take a deep breath in for three seconds, then forcefully expel it for seven seconds. Repeat this three to five times. Your child can do this standing up, sitting, or lying down—whatever is most comfortable for them.

   What to say and do. You can describe the process like this: "Put your hand on your tummy. Now, take a very big, deep breath in while I count to three, then push it out as hard as you can while I count to seven." For younger children, simply tell them to copy you taking a deep breath in and forcing the air out, as they may not be able to follow your counting.

   You can also first show them what to do. Demonstrate the deep breathing, then say, "Now, let's try this together, because it will make you feel so much better!" Practice doing this a few times until your child gets the hang of this exercise.

2. **Movement**

   Movement is especially beneficial to children, as it can help them release endorphins, serotonin, and adrenaline while also increasing their energy levels, which will help them focus on the Neurocycle.

   What to say and do. To begin this activity, pick a movement for you and your child to do for a few minutes, one that you know they will enjoy. You can also ask your child to pick a movement. Some examples are jumping jacks, skipping, dancing, wiggling feet or toes, or something as simple as walking around the living room. You and your child may feel awkward doing some of these movements, and that is okay. Laugh at yourselves, laugh with each other, and allow yourselves to be silly for a moment.

Ask your child to focus on how the movement feels in their body. Do they feel excited, tired, silly? This is like an active type of meditation for children that helps them focus on how their body feels. The more you do exercises like this, the more you will teach your child to be fully present within their body and put their focus on what they're doing in the moment.

This kind of intentional and directed movement is a way of helping your child redirect their thoughts from what they are struggling with by focusing on their body and what they can do with it. It's a really great way to get them ready for Step 1 of the Neurocycle, Gather Awareness.

This activity can go on as long as it needs to. The key is to move until you reach a point where you feel your child is in a calmer state of mind.

3. Creativity

Creativity is also a way to calm down the mind, brain, and body and decompress before or after working on the Neurocycle. Creativity is also an excellent, tangible way to release overwhelming emotions.

What to say and do. The first thing to do is ask your child to pick a creative activity they love to do. Some examples are drawing, painting, playing with playdough or LEGOs, and so on.

Ask your child to draw, color, paint, or shape three things that they love to do or three of their favorite memories. This creative visualization will help your child focus their attention on what brings them joy, which will in turn help them manage any emotions that feel overwhelming in the moment.

As your child creatively visualizes a happy thought or memory, they are building healthy neural networks into their brain that are like support systems or insurance policies they can fall back on in times of need. They are essentially building up their mental resilience!

Other examples of brain preparation / decompression activities include teaching your child positive affirmations, asking your child to repeat a quote or a prayer that is comforting to them, or listening to music or asking your child to play their instrument if that is something they enjoy. The list above is just a guide, as there are many possible decompression activities you can do with your child.

The key is to focus on what your child loves and what brings them joy and helps them calm down. Then you use this knowledge to create your own unique way of helping your child calm their mind, brain, and body so that they will be more focused and prepared to do the Neurocycle.

Try to avoid rushing the process or getting annoyed with your child if they are battling to focus or feeling emotional. The increasing rate of toxic electromagnetic energy in the mind and brain from such hurry and annoyance in an elevated situation will only grow unhealthy trees and compound the issue. This negative energy in and around us can pollute us and block clarity of mind in the situation.

8

∎∎∎∎∎∎∎

How to Do Step 1:
Gather Awareness

The Gather Awareness step helps children from a young age learn how to identify and name hard emotions, which diffuses the charge of the emotions and allows for more effective self-regulation.

Gather Awareness, Step 1 of the Neurocycle, is a deliberate type of awareness that focuses on *specific* information—it goes beyond general awareness. In the Gather Awareness step, you want to teach your child to zoom in and *specifically* focus on the four warning signals discussed in part 1: emotions, behaviors, bodily sensations, and perspectives. As your child does this, you will want to encourage them to ask a lot of what and how questions with the purpose of gaining

Brain-ee gathering the four warning signal branches

information that will help them understand what's going on in their mind and improving their mental health.

With children ages 3–6, you can use demonstration and enactment to walk them through Step 1 of the Neurocycle. I suggest decorating four boxes—shoeboxes work well—then filling them with pictures. The pictures in each box should represent one of the four warning signals. The first box is for pictures of feelings, such as Brain-ee and all the emotions, which you can get from the coloring book I created to go along with this book, or you can find pictures in magazines, in other coloring books, on the internet, and so on. Try to find pictures for many different emotions. Fill the second box with pictures of behaviors, such as throwing toys or crying. Again, you can cut these images from our Brain-ee coloring book or find them other places. The third box is for pictures of bodily reactions, such as pains in the body like an upset tummy or a sore head.

Instead of putting pictures in the fourth box representing perspectives—how someone is looking at life—you could put in two pairs of sunglasses. One pair can be colorful and pretty, and the other pair can be dark or broken. You can then ask your child to put on the pair of sunglasses that represents how they are seeing life at that moment, or how they are seeing this particular situation. Is it bad and scary, or do they think things will be okay?

For children ages 7–10, you can use pictures but also add words written on paper to your boxes. Perspective is often one of the hardest warning signals to explain to a child, so you can also show them the perspectives image of Brain-ee holding two pairs of sunglasses in chapter 3 to help your child understand what you mean.

In your boxes, it's important to have pictures of young children's faces as well as those of older children and adults. This will help your child understand that these problems happen to people of all ages. Other ideas of things you can put in the boxes are pictures you and your child drew together, objects, and toys.

Making these boxes can be a fun brain preparation activity that you do with your child before you start Neurocycling. It might also help get them engaged and more willing to do the Neurocycle; it makes the process more like a game and less like a chore or something they have to do.

Also, don't worry if it takes some time for your child to get the hang of this step. Recent research shows that children as young as ages 2–4 have a fairly insightful understanding of emotional concepts, much more so than we used to understand.[1] However, they often don't have the linguistic cues to fully describe and explain all these concepts, and that's where we come in as adults. We can help our children by providing words and giving them different ways of expressing themselves using movement, enactment, toys, pictures, music, storybooks, and so on.

Gather Awareness Action Steps

1. Using the Brain-ee Gather Awareness image at the beginning of this chapter, say something like, "We are going to find out what's on the branches of the messy thought tree in your brain that is making you sad."

2. Have the four warning signal boxes out and ready somewhere convenient in your house. Start opening one warning signal box at a time and help your child choose the picture or object that best represents how they feel emotionally and physically, their behavior, and their perspective.

3. If they get confused, remind them of Brain-ee picking up the branches, which are their warning signals. You prompt this process with questions. (For help, refer back to the four warning signals table in chapter 3.)

   For example, take a picture out of the emotions box of a sad face and ask your child if this is how they feel. You may have to go through all your pictures to find the emotion that best matches how they feel, or you may have to add an emotion—one quick way to do this is using a notepad and pen to draw a few faces. Tell them you will find or draw more pictures together later today if you need to. You can keep adding pictures as you find them or as your child develops a deeper understanding of their more complex emotions. The more pictures or objects you have that represent different emotions, the better!

Involve your child in this process from the beginning, and they may get to a point where they will start finding pictures or objects on their own to put into their boxes. Try to encourage them to do this regularly as they develop a sense of the complexity of their emotions—this will help them see that they have a safe space to process how they feel. With children ages 7–10, you can use the pictures with more words, or get your child to write how they feel—whatever works for them! You can do this with all four boxes.

4. Take blocks of about 5–15 minutes to do this. If your child needs more time, that's fine. If at any point they want to stop, this is also okay; just pick up where you left off later in the day or tomorrow. If your child gets upset, take a break and do a decompression activity with them to help them calm down (see chapter 7).

9

How to Do Step 2: Reflect

The Reflect step is vital, because the process makes the thought weaker so it can be changed.

What Is the Reflect Step?

The Reflect step is where you help your child seek the deeper meaning behind their four signals. You are essentially teaching your child how to examine the details of the signals, the branches on their thought tree, to find the why behind their emotions, behaviors, bodily sensations, and perspectives.

It helps to create a Reflect box that contains lots of pictures of *situations*. Some examples include an adult yelling at a child, a teacher in a

Brain-ee reflecting on his warning signals and trying to work out what they are telling him

75

classroom full of shouting kids, someone being bullied or teased, and so on. These are just some examples of what you can put in the Reflect box; you can also come up with other pictures or objects that would uniquely connect to how your child understands these concepts. This is an ongoing, organic process as your child finds more pictures and objects they like.

For children ages 6–10, you can have words and phrases written on paper as well. However, remember that it won't be possible to anticipate all potential situations, so add new ones as you work them out with your child. These are triggered by the incoming information from the current experience.

To explain this to your child, you can say that this is like when Brain-ee digs up the ground around the roots to expose them and find out what is going on. When the roots are exposed in this way, it shakes up the tree, and the unhealthy branches are loosened, which makes it easier to gather and analyze them to see how to make the tree better. This is a very important step because it makes the thought weaker so it can be changed.

Reflect Action Steps

1. Using the picture of Brain-ee at the beginning of this chapter and the images of the four warning signals in chapter 3, say something like, "Look how Brain-ee is staring at the branches. Well, that is what we are going to do to find out more details of what's going on so that we can see what is on the branches of the messy thought tree in your mind and understand what is making you feel sad, angry, scared, upset, confused—or however you feel."

2. Next, use the pictures your child chose from the warning signal boxes I spoke about in the Gather Awareness step to begin a process of ask, answer, and discuss. Use why, how, when, who, and where questions for each of the four signals. In this step, you are expanding on the information collected

in Step 1 and gaining more specific descriptions of the warning signals. Starting with emotions, for example, ask, "Why do you think you feel _____?"

Then provide some options for your child, because they may not have the words to describe why they feel a certain way. For example, you can ask them something like, "Do you feel sad because someone said something to you to make you feel sad? Yes? What did they say?" Then you can ask something like, "Can you use your toys to show me what happened? Or do you want to find a picture that shows me what happened?"

With children ages 3–6, you can use playacting or toys as you ask these questions. Sometimes it's easier for a child to make their favorite toy or imaginary friend answer a hard question, which creates distance between the child and what happened. They may do this spontaneously, or, if your child is battling to answer, you can try this approach. If you have the Brain-ee toy, you can use the toy with your child.

3. Then focus on the behavioral warning signals and repeat the process above by saying something like, "I see that when you feel sad, you don't want to play because [describe whatever you worked out with the emotional warning signals]." As you do this, you are helping your child make connections between the signals. The more you do this with them, the more they will start doing it on their own.

4. Next, move on to the bodily sensation warning signals. Show them the pictures of Brain-ee and repeat the process above with questions like, "How is the sadness [or other emotion] feeling in your body? Does your tummy hurt or do your shoulders feel tight because you feel sad?" Use lots of demonstrations and act it out together.

5. Last, focus on the perspective warning signals and ask them to put on whatever pair of sunglasses they think best shows

how they are viewing or understanding their experience. You can also ask them to point to one of the pairs of sunglasses Brain-ee is holding in the perspectives image in chapter 3 or ask them to explain or act out how what has happened makes them feel toward their friends, school, siblings, family, or themselves.

6. Take a block of about 5–15 minutes to do this. If your child needs more time, that's fine. You can also use the tips from the Gather Awareness chapter to help your child understand how to do this step.

7. If at any point they want to stop, this is also okay; just pick up where you left off later in the day or tomorrow. If your child gets upset, take a break and do a decompression activity with them to help them calm down (see chapter 7). Don't push your child—always have an open-door policy that creates a safe space for them to process their emotions in their own time.

8. For all ages, focus on helping them express themselves by rewording or expanding their sentences and then asking, "Is this what you are going through? If not, can you help me understand?" This will make your child feel heard and validated and help them feel like they have a safe, nonjudgmental space to speak.

10

How to Do Step 3: Write/Play/Draw

Writing and drawing bring order out of chaos by "putting the mind on paper." This is an incredibly important step, because if we don't help our children get their suppressed thoughts out, they will stay rooted and can cause more mental and physical distress.

What Is the Write/Play/Draw Step?

The Write/Play/Draw step often goes hand in hand with the Reflect step. While the Reflect step helps reveal the why behind the signals, the Write/Play/Draw step helps reveal the how, when, who, and where.

The Write/Play/Draw step is a very revealing process. It pulls the memories of the thoughts out into the open, which adds clarity and brings suppressed thoughts out of the nonconscious mind. Your child may

Brain-ee writing down his signals and reflections

remember things they were not consciously aware were bothering them or were linked in some way to how they are reacting and behaving.

Writing and drawing bring order out of chaos by "putting the mind on paper." This is an incredibly important step, because if we don't help our children get their suppressed thoughts out, they will stay rooted and can cause more mental and physical distress. For younger kids, playacting or using toys can also be a way for them to "write"—that is, to express and clarify their thoughts. This can also help you better understand what they are going through as you help them work through the Neurocycle process.

Write/Play/Draw Action Steps

1. The point of Step 3 is to help capture and expand on whatever your child discovered about the four warning signals as they did Steps 1 and 2, so it's a good idea to do this step quite soon after the other two steps, or alongside Step 2.

2. Using the image of Brain-ee writing at the beginning of this chapter and the images of the four warning signals in chapter 3, say something like, "We are going to write, play, and draw with Brain-ee today—this is how we will help your brain find what is making you sad [or another feeling]." Your child can write down their thoughts in a notebook or on paper, or if they prefer, they can draw a picture that depicts everything they just uncovered or playact what they are trying to express. However, it is important that your child understands this is different from a decompression activity. Whatever they choose to do, they should deliberately and intentionally focus on what they are expressing and why.

3. Encourage your child to write down or draw whatever comes up into their conscious mind, even if it seems like it doesn't make sense at that exact moment. Encourage your child to

pour their thoughts out. Don't worry about making it neat and tidy! They can sort it out in the Recheck step. Writing plays a massive role in organizing thinking and activating the two sides of the brain, even if it may look a bit messy at first.

11

How to Do Step 4: Recheck

This step is designed to help your child accept the experience—what happened to them—while empowering them to reconceptualize it so that it no longer controls how they feel and function.

What Is the Recheck Step?

In this step, you are helping your child redesign their story and repair the messy roots of their thought tree so that it no longer has a negative effect on their mental health. This step is designed to help your child accept the experience—what happened to them—while empowering them to reconceptualize it so that it no longer controls how they feel and function. It will teach your child to think about what happened to them in a new light: *Yes, this happened to me, and it is affecting how I am*

Brain-ee working out how to make his thought tree healthy

83

thinking, feeling, and behaving, but what can I do about it? How can I mend my story? How can I make this thought tree healthy?

At this time, remember to include looking at the impact of your child's coping mechanisms on others. This will help your child understand that how they think and react to life will also impact their relationships, which is part of empathy development and self-regulation.

Recheck Action Steps

1. Show your child the image of Brain-ee rechecking his thoughts at the beginning of this chapter. You can say something like, "We are going to work out how we can see this thought tree differently. Yes, this happened, but what can we do to make it better? What can we mend this thought tree with to make it healthy?"

2. There are two ways you can visualize this step with your child. First, if there is an established pattern that is originating from a painful trauma or toxic experience, this can be visualized as an ugly looking tree that is poisonous or has thorns and is causing damage to the surrounding soil and other thought trees. In this case, your child has to dig up the thought tree and fix the roots of the tree so that it stops growing thorns and poisoning the ground.

   Once this has been done, your child will put the thought tree back into the soil, and it will regrow in a more beautiful way—it will become a healthy thought tree. This is a good way to explain the process of reconceptualization to your child. The memory of what happened to them is a part of their story and will never go away. They aren't cutting down the tree or planting a new one to cover it up, but they also don't want the poison to take over or for the tree to stay like it is. This is why, in Step 4, they are fixing how the tree grows. They are turning it into something that isn't harming their ability to get through life. They are getting rid of those painful, poisonous thorns that hurt them and mending the thought tree so that it regrows into something that won't cause so much pain when they think about it.

The replanted thought tree is characterized by a sense of acceptance—they are at peace with the past. This is represented in the image of Brain-ee looking at a tree with a wilted side and a leafy green side. The old story is connected to the newly reconceptualized thought. However, this new leafy green side is bigger and more powerful, while the old story stays there as a shadow of the past—it is no longer poisoning the tree.

Brain-ee looking happily at the new
healthy thought tree—the old story
is now weak and has no power!

The second way to visualize this process is for toxic things that have happened that are not on the same level as a major trauma. Although these experiences can feel distressful in the moment, they aren't as strong or developed as traumatic experiences and are much less disruptive to our well-being. The image here is a tree that has wilting leaves, broken branches, and some roots that are rotting. There may even be some bugs eating the tree. These are all the things that have happened that showed up in the Gather Awareness, Reflect, and Write/Play/Draw steps.

As your child goes through the Recheck step, they are getting rid of these bugs, dead leaves, broken branches, and rotting roots by pruning the tree, adding fertilizer to the soil, and watering the tree. Now, as the reconceptualized tree grows, it has healthy green leaves. The memory of the broken, unhealthy thought tree is still there, but it's just a faded image that shows the old story that used to hurt them and make them worried and scared. This old, unhealthy thought tree no longer has any power over them.

3. Your child can work through this process by reviewing what they wrote or drew in Step 3 and explaining what they see. They can then add more pictures, drawings, and information to it, sorting out the information by using arrows, circles, boxes, or anything else they want to use to bring more clarity and organization to their thinking. This is the "pulling up the roots and healing the leaves" process.

As your child does this, you can help them see how their story has impacted them *and* other people by changing how they feel, what they say and do, how this made them feel in their body, and how it made them act toward others. You can use the images of the four warning signals (chapter 3) to help them talk about what they were doing and how their experiences were affecting them.

You can also help them demonstrate this by filling a glass with water to overflowing or filling a balloon with water until it bursts—this is what it feels like to have that unhealthy thought tree in their brain. You could even build a mini volcano together as an exercise and tell them that the exploding "lava" represents their warning signals and that the way to stop it from exploding is by making the thought tree healthy.

4. Next, help them see the impact of their coping mechanisms—the warning signals—on their life as well as the lives of the people they love, and how they could act differently. For example, their meltdown made them feel really horrible and confused and made the people they love—a parent, sibling, or friend—sad for them. Emphasize that it isn't their fault that other people were affected, but because people love them, how they act will impact other people.

    This exercise isn't designed to make your child feel guilty or punish them. It's meant to teach them to be self-aware and to understand that what they say and do will affect the people in their life—and this can be both a good and a bad thing. It is important to have self-awareness with relation to other people. This is an important part of self-regulation and empathy development.

5. At this point in the step, congratulate your child for all their good work. Emphasize that it's great that they have said all these things. Tell them how it isn't easy to talk about emotions and that you are going to work out what to do about this together—they are not alone. This will give your child a sense of control and autonomy and help them feel validated.

6. You can then talk about looking for other, more effective ways to perceive or see the situation so that its impact on their life is neutralized. This is the "making the thought tree healthy" step. This won't take the struggle away, but it will help them manage it and work out a way forward.

    For example, if your child is struggling at school and this is making them upset, you can say something like, "It's okay to struggle to learn how to read. These kinds of struggles are normal, and we all have different things we struggle with. But it won't help if you ignore how you feel or avoid learning how to read, even if you are struggling. This is why we want to make things better—we want to make that thought tree stronger and healthy."

We don't want our children to think that it's okay to get attached or chained to negative coping strategies such as running away from or avoiding an issue. We need to help our children create a language and a context that give them the ability to face their struggles and overcome them, even if it takes time.

7. This is where you will help your child look for antidotes or ways to make the thought tree healthy. Reconceptualization is, at its core, a way of finding alternative perspectives to counteract the painful elements of a story and experience. Once this origin story is clearer—what you have been doing with your child up to this point—then you can help them find an alternative way of looking at the issue.

You are helping your child change the "pain energy" from what happened to "recovery energy" they can use to make this better. You are essentially taking the sting out of the story—it's still emotional but is managed emotion. Of course, the thought tree will take time to heal, and you can show them this by taking their hand and taking small steps forward while saying, "This is what progress looks like, one little step at a time. This is how we make our thought trees healthy." You can then help them look for antidotes to help them make these steps.

In the example above, this could include explaining to your child that accepting their difficulty with reading doesn't mean they are bad or stupid and that everyone in life battles with different things. You can tell your child that you will help them learn how to read; there are many ways to learn, and you will help them find the best way for them. You can even suggest ways to talk about what they are going through, such as, "Tell your friends that there is a small hurt in your brain that is getting healed so you will be able to read. Just like when you fall and hurt yourself, it takes time to get better."

8. One great activity to demonstrate the Recheck step is to have a box of items you don't mind being broken, such as crayons, toys, foods, or building blocks. You can also use plates, vases, or cups, but these have the potential to cause your child injury, so I recommend using softer items that can't hurt them when broken. Allow your child to throw an item on the floor in a designated area of your home under your supervision, which will help release pent-up energy. Then help them gather up the pieces and sit together as you rebuild the item. You can even use child-safe glue that has glitter in it, or tape that is colorful and has pictures. This is called the kintsugi principle, which is the Japanese art of repairing broken pottery and vases with glue that has gold, silver, or platinum in it. The idea is to embrace flaws, imperfections, and the messiness that happens when life propels us in haphazard directions and grow from them. If you are using a food item such as a cookie or waffle, you can use colorful icing or syrup to help it stick together.

When you are finished, admire this new item and explain how the things that happen to us can make us feel broken, but when we Neurocycle, we fix the brokenness and make what happened to us better—the new thought tree is beautiful in a new way. Yes, it's different, but it's actually better. The cracks filled with beauty show what we went through to get here.

I recommend doing this activity only a few times, as it can be quite time-consuming and messy. If possible, keep the rebuilt item in a special place to remind your child that they got through something hard once and made it better, which means that they can get through the next challenge too.

12

■■■■■■■■

How to Do Step 5:
Active Reach

Active Reach is a great way to help your child develop their mental resilience. It's a purposeful distraction that will lift your child's mood and discipline their messy mind, helping them stay in a positive place throughout the day.

What Is the Active Reach Step?

Active Reach is the final step of the Neurocycle.

Active Reach involves creating a brief, self-encouraging statement that is followed by a simple, pleasant action and practicing it multiple times a day to strengthen the reconceptualized thought tree. Its purpose is twofold:

I can do it!

Brain-ee practicing
the Active Reach

1. To keep your child from slipping back and ruminating on the issue as they progress through the day.

91

2. To wire the reconceptualized thought tree into the brain until it becomes a very strong thought tree that influences your child's thinking and behavior—a habit.

Your child's Active Reaches will change progressively as they gain more insight into their thoughts. Your child may want to do the same Active Reach for a few days at a time and then add to it, or change it completely as they learn more about their thinking.

Active Reach is a great way to help your child practice their new way of thinking about the issue and develop their mental resilience. It's a purposeful distraction that will lift your child's mood and discipline their messy mind, helping them stay in a positive place throughout the day. It will help your child avoid self-preoccupation, which can increase feelings of depression and anxiety.[1]

Active Reach Action Steps

1. Use the image of Brain-ee doing an Active Reach at the beginning of this chapter to encourage your child. Remind them that with their Neurocycle superpower, they can do this!

2. It may help if you take the lead and work out a few Active Reaches for your child for the day that incorporate all the elements they worked on in Steps 1–4. You can suggest a couple of options that they can choose from, which they may choose to change.

3. An Active Reach also serves as a feedback and monitoring process, which will help your child develop their self-regulation and mindful awareness skills. Active Reaches are not set in stone; they are ways for your child to examine how they feel and pivot if necessary. You want your child to ask things like, *I tried something—did it work? Do I feel better?* If yes, then encourage them to carry on in that direction. If

not, then encourage them to ask, *What else can I do? I will keep trying things until something works.* Each day, encourage your child to check their Active Reach from the day before to see if they want to keep the same one or change it. If they want to change their Active Reach, tell them that even though it may not have been exactly the right thing, it got them moving in the right direction.

4. Your child should take around 3–5 minutes to make their Active Reach and about 1 minute to practice it. They can take a little longer if they feel the need to, especially if they are using a decompression activity to deal with a trigger. If they need to take a break, that's fine—they can repeat the Active Reach step during the day as needed.

5. Your child should practice their Active Reach each time they feel drawn back into ruminating on the issue or feel triggered. If neither of these things happen, it's still a good idea to consciously and deliberately practice working through the Active Reach with your child at least seven times a day, which will help strengthen the newly reconceptualized thought tree. I recommend setting a reminder on your phone or other device to do this with your child.

If you desire, you can also download the Neurocycle app and complete the 63-day Neurocycle with your child virtually. The Neurocycle app (available in your iOS or Android app store) offers an extension of the process outlined in this chapter and the previous four chapters, including guided introductions to each of the 5 Steps. Additionally, each day's Neurocycle describes the changes that are occurring in the brain daily, a unique brain preparation technique, and the option to be reminded to do the Active Reach, with seven daily notifications set at your frequency preference.

13

■■■■■■■■

The Timing of the Neurocycle

The most important thing to remember is that it takes 63 days to change a thought and build a habit, not 21 days.

The Neurocycle is designed to work in cycles of 63 days. It isn't an instant process. It allows for the rational and systematic evaluation of toxic events and circumstances within controlled time frames, which helps wire in new neural networks that lead to empowered mind-management. It takes time to create and stabilize a new, reconceptualized thought—a new, healthy thought tree—that leads to actual change.

The Neurocycle is the process that will help your child transition their dominant, disruptive thinking patterns *over time* into new, stabilized thoughts with embedded memories. In short, it is designed to help your child create new, sustainable habits in repeated cycles of 63 days that will produce behavior change in their life and build

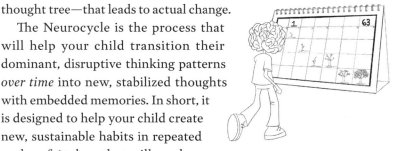

Brain-ee counting how many days he has done the Neurocycle

up their resilience. One full cycle is needed *per* issue that you want to work on with your child.

The Two Main Time Frames of the Neurocycle System

The Neurocycle system

There are two main time frames of the Neurocycle system:

1. **Established patterns like trauma and toxic habits.** To change the neural wiring of established patterns or change unhealthy thought trees, the Neurocycle needs to be used daily in cycles of 63 days.

2. **A moment of crisis or as needed.** You can use the Neurocycle as a mind-management hack to calm down the mind, brain, and body and get clarity in the moment. The more your child practices this, the easier it will be for them to do the 63-day cycles for establishing habits and repairing traumas.

When it comes to *established patterns*, it's really important to avoid trying to solve everything in one day. It's better to work in short bursts of time over the course of 63 days, which will lead to more effective and stable neural rewiring—building new thought trees.[1]

Ideally, this will involve doing the 5 Steps of the Neurocycle daily for around 7–15 minutes for 63 days. For example, if your child is moving schools or homes, or experiencing major changes in the family unit or with friends, it will take around 63 days to adapt. In the first 21 days of using the Neurocycle daily, we *start* seeing changes in thinking or behavior. However, to make sure that these changes are sustainable, you will need to remember to help your child practice using the Neurocycle for another 42 days.

Your child can do this by attaching the action to a task they already do daily, such as saying their Active Reach statement while brushing their hair or getting dressed. This will remind them to think about the new thought daily. Remember, to practice the new thought, your child should do Active Reaches seven times throughout the day.

In more extreme situations that involve traumas such as abuse or bullying, your child may need more than one 63-day cycle. Every situation will have its own set of challenges. The more complex the trauma, the more associated toxic issues may come up, and the more time you will need to spend doing the Neurocycle with your child.[2]

Other situations are more manageable, such as an *in the moment* mental health issue or minor crisis. Your child may get frustrated because they don't want to go to bed, they may be upset after fighting with their siblings, or they may throw a tantrum at a store because they want to leave. In these kinds of situations, you can go through the Neurocycle with them quickly and do the 5 Steps in around 1–5 minutes.

Be Patient and Flexible

The most important thing to remember is that it takes 63 days to change a thought and build a habit, not 21 days. Twenty-one has consistently been touted as the "magic" number of days to build habits and change behaviors, yet real change takes much longer, especially if the behavior is entrenched or established.[3] Actual changes in how we show up are created slowly as we reconceptualize thoughts and their associated behaviors in a stable and organized way over small amounts of time, which is why the Neurocycle is designed to be used daily in cycles of 63 days. It takes weeks, not days, to form new neural pathways, which are where the thought tree "lives."

Many adults and children fall back into old patterns of thinking and acting because they don't know the length of time that is needed to deconstruct an old thought and reconstruct a new thought in its place. My research and other studies have shown that it takes an average of 63 to 66 days for a new habit to form that will show up as a change in someone's life.[4] As mentioned above, sometimes it can even take multiple 63-day cycles to see change, depending on the complexity of the trauma or toxic habit. You can explain this time frame to your child using the images below.

The Thought Tree at Day 1   The Thought Tree at Day 21   The Thought Tree at Day 63

The key thing to remember as you work through the Neurocycle with your child is *flexibility*. Even though there is a time frame attached to the process of mind-management, you will need to be flexible with young children. Try not to be too regimented and try to be patient with yourself and your child. This whole system is designed and structured to help *reduce* stress, not increase stress.

The estimated times for each Neurocycle are based on the science of neuroplasticity and mind-management. They are also based on how long children ages 3–10 can realistically focus on mental health issues. While children ages 7–10 may be closer to the fifteen-minute mark, those ages 3–6 will probably be closer to the five-minute mark.

However, there are always exceptions! Some days things may be going so well that you go longer, maybe even up to forty-five minutes. Some days you won't get past Gather Awareness in fifteen minutes. Some days you will whiz through all 5 Steps in five minutes. Other days you may do only the decompression activity or get stuck on a certain step. It might be that all you get done in a day, or even in a few days, is acknowledging that something is going on and just hugging your child and leaving it there until the next day. This will especially be the case as you start introducing the Neurocycle into your lifestyle and getting into a routine.

As you work through the Neurocycle process with your child, try not to go beyond forty-five minutes in one sitting because the mind-management process can be draining—unless, of course, you're doing one of the related creative activities suggested earlier. You will need to schedule additional time for some of these activities, such as making the warning signal boxes, or any activities you think up yourself. Make these fun and interactive, which will help your child enjoy the Neurocycle process more.

It's also important not to let your child get preoccupied with the negative. Remember, always try to end the process on a constructive note, as this will help keep the neuroplasticity of the brain and the conscious mind moving in a hopeful direction.[5] Use this superhero Brain-ee image to frequently encourage your child throughout the Neurocycle.

What Do Things Look Like after 63 Days?

As your child goes through the 63 days, they will learn how to re-conceptualize the situation associated with the main toxic thought tree, which means they won't have anything holding them to that toxic thought tree anymore, like Brain-ee in the image above at day 63. Even though the old thought is still there, it's completely different: it's small and weak and has lost its power.

At the end of this process, the new thought is in control. The time your child spent over the 63 days growing the new thought tree and stabilizing it means the old thought won't be popping up all the time and impacting their thoughts and actions. Over time, using the Neurocycle, your child will have weakened the old thought tree in a systematic way; therefore, it will have lost its power to control them.

Establishing a Routine

Establishing a routine is really important as you work through the Neurocycle with your child. Doing something at the same location and time of day (as much as possible) can help both you and your child form new habits, reduce stress, and manage your mental health.[6]

Having a routine will also help build up your child's self-regulation and resilience. The more they practice the Neurocycle, the more their mind-management skills will become automatized, which means they will be able to carry them over into other situations that arise during their day.[7] Over time, this will decrease their dependency on willpower and motivation, which tend to drop when we are in the throes of a highly emotional or reactive state.[8] It's exhausting to repeatedly struggle to control our actions and do the right thing—as we adults know only too well!

Automatization is incredibly important. It will help your child get to the point where, when they find themselves in a situation similar to what triggered them before, they respond differently. It may *feel* like they are responding without thinking, but this isn't the case. On the contrary, it means that the new, healthy thought tree has been wired into the brain by their mind over sufficient time, which has changed its structure so that it is more stable and can therefore be used in a new way (as a new behavior pattern). Going back to the image of the storm in the thought tree forest, this new thought tree is strong enough to withstand the storm and offer shelter. Yes, something bad is happening, but now your child is more confident because they know how to handle the situation.

Think about teaching your child to ride a bicycle. Your child goes from not being able to balance on the bike, to riding it with training wheels, to riding it without training wheels without consciously thinking about what they are doing. However, behind the scenes, a lot is happening. Intelligent, dynamic self-regulation is occurring in your child's mind and in the neural networks of their brain to build this thought tree into an automatized habit. I discuss this learning process in depth in my book *Think, Learn, Succeed*. Now, as your child confidently rides their bike, they are *not* thinking. Their mind, brain, and body are following a pattern of thinking that has been established over time through practice, which is what is also happening as you work through the Neurocycle with your child. Talk about having a superpower! The mind and brain are truly incredible.

PART 3

APPLYING THE NEUROCYCLE TO LIFE EXPERIENCES

Here's the Neurocycle applied to five different and common challenges for children. This part of the book is designed to help you help your child develop the type of autonomy that leads to mental resilience and improved mental health.

14

Trauma

As much as trauma changes us and can result in mental and physical damage, we also have the power to change what these traumatic stories look like inside our brain, body, and mind.

The experience of trauma is vastly different for each person, and the healing process is also different. There's no magic solution that can help everyone, and it takes time, work, and the willingness to face what is uncomfortable for true healing to take place, as hard as this can be. Thankfully, there's no deadline when it comes to overcoming trauma—each person can do it in a way that works for them. Trauma has a different pattern in the mind and brain than a toxic habit. Trauma is involuntary and has been inflicted on a person, which often leaves the person feeling emotionally and physically exposed, worn-out, and fearful.

To help you better understand what trauma is, I want to tell you a story about a wonderful and brave eight-year-old child, who we will call Tim, and his amazing parents and sister. Their story covers many topics discussed in part 4 and will help you see what using the Neurocycle looks like with real-life issues. Before you read this story, however, I want to note that it includes mention of physical, emotional, and sexual abuse and may be hard for some readers. Feel free to move on to a different chapter or come back to this section when you feel you are ready.

I have divided the story into three parts: Mom's story, Tim's story, and Dad's story. This will enable you to see what happened from three different perspectives, which, in turn, will help you better understand what happens when you use the Neurocycle with your child and how to facilitate the three keys of communication discussed in chapter 5 to improve both your child's mental resilience and your relationship.

Mom's Story

My family's story with the Neurocycle begins with my son's many struggles with sleep and nervous issues following his early life trauma. My husband and I received full custody of our son, Tim, when he was four years old. Under his birth mother's custody, he had experienced many kinds of trauma, including physical abuse, feeding and hygiene neglect, medical care withholding, and sexual abuse.

These events resulted in him undergoing multiple corrective surgeries and many years of therapies, including therapy for a speech delay, occupational therapy for sensory processing and coordination delay issues, and counseling for behavioral issues and trauma processing.

Despite all these treatments, our son continued to struggle with sleep and behavioral issues. He would sleep no more than four nonconsecutive hours per night, frantically complaining of hot flashes, leg pains, and nightmares. He struggled with nightly, sometimes multiple, episodes of incontinence as well.

The behavioral struggles resulting from such irregular sleep and his background made it impossible for Tim to attend traditional school successfully. Weekly, we were called into his school for complaints about his lack of focus, disruptive verbal behaviors, aggression with other children, defiance in completing his work, and inability to comply with regular commands and rules.

At home, he struggled to follow more than one-step directions, remember basic daily tasks, and emotionally adjust to extracurricular activities with other kids, such as music or sports. Socially, this left him with few friends and struggling to find a place where he was understood or belonged. At this point, we decided to homeschool him so he could receive the attention and treatment he needed to develop a healthy physical, social, and mental existence.

His father and I searched high and low to resolve his issues. If there was a physical product on the market designed to help kids sleep, we bought it. His room was full of heavy blankets, sound machines, diffusers, and a host of other accoutrements. These managed to improve his sleep only a small amount, so we turned to medical practices. We saw sleep specialists to rule out sleep disorders, GI specialists to rule out gut to brain issues, chiropractors to rule out structural issues, brain balance specialists to rule out endocrine issues, and nutritionists to rule out dietary issues, and we tried hosts of holistic and homeopathic things in between to treat his nervous and social issues.

Nothing resolved these problems for him, and the strain on our family was immense. There was no scheduling anything after 6:00 p.m., as we needed to be home for our son's lengthy relaxation routine just to get him to sleep. There was no consistent sleeping after that, as his door alarm would go off three to six times per night as he woke and got up for something or for attention.

Finally, exhausted and out of options, we turned to psychiatric prescriptions. Over the course of a year, our son was placed on serious medications ranging from Ambien to Klonopin, restless leg medications to all manner of ADHD medications, and more, totaling over ten different combinations of day and night drugs. While he finally began sleeping eight to ten hours some nights, he was also constantly exhausted, drowsy, and overall low in demeanor.

While he was less disruptive in his behaviors, he continued to struggle. His sleep remained inconsistent as well, and he was still unable to cope with going back to sleep once he woke, even with all that medication. We operated like this with no other recourse for nearly a year before we happened, by what seemed like a fated chance, upon the Neurocycle.

Four days into the Neurocycle, we noticed a change in our son. He was able to self-soothe and return to sleep within ten minutes of waking in the night. His nightmares stopped. He seemed bright and happy during the day. It was an incredibly obvious differ-ence. Our son, who would never sleep past 7:00 a.m. under any circumstances, was able to sleep in. We were able to have a life as a family after 6:00 p.m., and everyone could appreciate the way this lifted the pall of stress surrounding bedtime over our house.

After 21 days, we were certain that this could replace his medi-cations, which never truly worked as they were billed to begin with. Over the remaining 42 days of the 63-day cycle, we tapered off all his nighttime medications. We were thrilled to notice that he continued to sleep an average of ten hours, was able to nearly always put himself back to sleep, maintained nightmare-free sleep, and was able to go to bed at variable times and sleep in if he went to bed late. The changes in his daily life were clear too. His attitude was better, tasks that had bred meltdowns and were unable to be done without constant reminding could now be completed quickly and independently, and his social skills improved.

The Neurocycle has become a staple of our family life now. Anytime our son struggles with a behavioral issue, we use the 5 Steps to bring him back into focus and clarity of attitude. The language that Tim learned to describe himself, his body, and how it functions has brought him great peace of mind in handling his traumas and nervous issues.

Now we don't need to use negative language about nontarget behaviors; instead, we can use transformative language to encour-age him to identify what warning signal he's experiencing, why it is coming out in a way that isn't appropriate, and what it needs to tell him about his feelings and behavioral needs. Additionally, the many breathing techniques he has acquired are helpful when destructive worries and emotions begin to take him over.

As parents, we've found that the language, techniques, and steps of the Neurocycle have helped us to manage our own emotions and behaviors when interacting with our son as well, creating a much-improved family environment. It's much easier to mete out proper responses and discipline when you understand where your child is biochemically and biophysically coming from and the real and effective channels to change the problem behavior.

Beyond helping us understand our son, the Neurocycle has also helped us understand our own reactions and their origin stories too. Even though children are innocent in the emotional strain parenting creates, it's still a very traumatic experience without a coping outlet for parents,

> **The Neurocycle has become a staple of our family life now. Anytime our son struggles with a behavioral issue, we use the 5 Steps to bring him back into focus and clarity of attitude.**

especially for parents of children with special needs. Listening to the Neurocycle alongside Tim helped me to properly attribute my toxic ideas about my relationship with my son.

All the ideas of *What am I doing to deserve these reactions from him? Why doesn't he appreciate me?* and *How can we keep going like this for the next ____ years?* began to settle into the appropriate truths that my output isn't always what determines my son's behavior, I don't need others' appreciation to do my best, and my positive relationship with my son is worth more than concerns about how long it will take. The process has continued to help me notice my warning signals before they become toxic emotions and has provided me with the brain preparation and breathing tools I need to manage my own parenting behaviors. As an additional benefit, watching me try to better myself with my Neurocycle seemed to motivate my son to work on his Neurocycle, and doing it together has been a bonding experience.

Tim's Story

I've been having problems. I've had sleep issues and anger problems. The breathing makes me feel nice and calm. It's helped me with a lot of stuff. When I Neurocycle, it helps me with my sleep and my behavior.

I love all the MPA [Multiple Perspective Advantage] stuff. It helps me with my day. I also love doing it every day. Sometimes I just want to do it again. Sometimes when I'm sad or angry or just feeling uncomfortable, I Neurocycle. Sometimes, when I miss a day, I work harder the next day. I also like it because if you're stressed from school or something, what you are stressed about will go away a lot, or even go away all the way. It's very fun too. If you get bored, you should just Neurocycle.

Dad's Story

From a very early age, Tim struggled with sleep and behavioral management. The mention of bedtime and beginning to put him in bed would start inconsolable crying that required hours of attention to soothe. Even once asleep, he was easily woken and experienced the same difficulty falling back asleep. His speech and social development were very slow, and he struggled to communicate in more than two-word utterances well into his fourth year.

The causes for these issues were unclear until he was about four years old. From birth, I had limited custody of Tim, who resided with his birth mother entirely during his first year of life, during which time she denied me access to him. When Tim was three, about to turn four, I was made aware Tim had been experiencing abuse. My wife and I were heartbroken and immediately fought for full custody of Tim and won.

Years of therapies, home adjustments, medications, and burnout ensued. My wife and I had to constantly battle his past trauma while trying to provide him with a normal childhood experience. It would seem like something was working for a few days only for the new tool or technique to lose its effect the next day. I began to tell my wife that we needed to stop focusing on therapies and treatments and live a normal life. The stress impacted our relationship with each other and with Tim, and it affected our daughter's (Tim's half sister) homelife too.

One day, my wife brought home the Neurocycle app. I didn't think much of it at first because we had tried other kinds of mindfulness, children's meditation, and recordings with Tim before. However, it became very clear that Tim didn't see this the same. Within a few days, he was talking positively about his sleep throughout the day, about fighting his nightmares, and about how he could get better. His Active Reaches visibly helped recalibrate his day and his mindset. After the first 63-day cycle, we were all able to sleep fully because he didn't wake throughout the night. I had always hated using medications, and it was a great relief when my wife and I were able to take him off them as well.

More than just providing such good nighttime effects, the Neurocycle gave us the language and steps to create a shared vocabulary to describe our mutual and individual experiences. We were able to verbalize the reasons for breathing sessions, Tim was able to understand why we asked him to think in a certain way, and everyone's behavior improved. When he deregulated, we could ask him to Neurocycle either with us or independently with the recordings in the app, and the improvement in his mood and behavior was instantly apparent.

The Neurocycle steps and language are a staple in our daily homelife. They give us a place to meet each other, improve our relationships, and help Tim recover his childhood and future with less familial stress and burnout. The terminology and focus on brain development and healing help our parent-child bond because we can remove ourselves from the immediate behavior and look to the long-term or bigger picture.

How This Story Can Help You

As much as trauma changes us and can result in mental and physical damage, we also have the power to change what these traumatic stories look like inside our brain, body, and mind.

Trauma comes from many areas, some of which include physical disabilities; major illnesses; extreme physical injury; grief; sexual, verbal, and emotional abuse; and societal issues such as poverty, racism, sexism, and homophobia, among other things. When it comes to dealing with extreme trauma in young children, the main point is to help them realize it's not their fault and they did nothing wrong. Creating a safe space where they can tell you absolutely anything as it comes back to them or when they are triggered is incredibly important.

It's also important not to be shocked or to tell your child to stop saying things that may make you feel uncomfortable. As you listen, you can gently explain why certain behaviors and emotions are inappropriate and show them healthier responses to their emotions that will help them feel better. Remember, your child's experience has been distorted by an extreme situation, and they are trying to cope in the only way that allows them to make some sense of it. They are trying to process what adults, other children, or strangers in their life did to them, or whatever other traumatic event they experienced, that distorted their perspective, even if this "making sense" is just accepting that what happened doesn't make sense. Just being able to share their story in a safe space is a huge step in the healing process.

This is why the Neurocycle is so helpful. It provides a systematic and safe way to help your child talk about and process their story.

Introspection opens the doorway to what I call "the wise mind," which helps turn all those unhealthy thought trees into new, healthy, green thought trees. This is what we saw in Tim's story.

As I explained in part 1, thoughts and their embedded memories form a body-wide interactive network. It takes uncomfortable, hard work and a *significant amount* of time to consciously access a thought tree in the nonconscious mind and deconstruct it down to the root level. To use the analogy Tim used when telling me about his experience using the Neurocycle, "The first three steps are like a bee taking pollen from a flower, and it then spreads the pollen around, and lots of new flowers grow—this part is like what the Recheck and Active Reach do."

The science of the impact of traumatic early childhood experiences is well-established. We now know that, without positive intervention and mind-management, a child experiencing periodic or continuous encounters that cause toxic stress can suffer damage to the structure and function of their mind, brain, and body, which will manifest in their body and how they live their life.[1]

Trauma reorders neural networks, thoughts, and sensory pathways so that a person's mind, brain, and body will continue to respond as if they were in a really dangerous situation even when they are not.[2] This is called trauma response; it's a coping mechanism developed in reaction to the trauma but isn't generally the best thing for the child in the long term.

This is why the Neurocycle is so helpful. It provides a systematic and safe way to help your child talk about and process their story.

This is where mind-management and the Neurocycle come in. Whatever we think about most grows, and whatever grows manifests in how we behave toward ourselves and others. Unfortunately, unmanaged trauma in the nonconscious mind also grows the longer it is unattended, becoming big, messy thought trees that influence how we function.

Trauma can distort memories in ways that can mask the messages from the nonconscious mind, whose role it is to alert the conscious mind to what's going on through its warning signals.[3] It's almost as though the conscious mind becomes blurry, like a pair of sunglasses misting up, making them difficult to see through. In this state of mind, our ability to think clearly and use discernment is reduced, which makes it easy to react negatively to information, people, and different situations.

We see this in Tim's story. No one can predict how a traumatized child will express their unmanaged toxic stress. However, if left unmanaged, this stress has the potential to grow out of control, which can lead to behavioral issues, the inability to connect socially, physical symptoms, lack of sleep, learning problems, and so on. This is why it's imperative that we help children learn how to manage their mind from a young age.

Trauma, the Mind, and the Brain

The mind and brain are organized for survival. This means that when we get into a difficult situation, the mind and brain are designed to help. We can change the disordered neural networks *with* the mind. There is always hope!

Below is a simplified way of looking at how neural networks—thoughts—can become disordered as well as the changes that happen in the brain as a child is experiencing a trauma. The first image

Healthy thought trees   Thought trees with trauma

is of a healthy thought tree. The second is of a toxic thought tree that could represent a trauma.

A toxic experience can lead to a messy mind, and this messiness goes into the brain as messy energy, which affects how the different parts of the brain work in response. It's as if not all the thought tree's parts, or the axons and dendrites, properly communicate with each other, which is shown by the blacked-out portion in the unhealthy tree above.

In the image below, you can see some of the different areas of the brain that are affected by trauma. Although trauma can impact the whole brain—through many complicated processes—for simplicity's sake, I will just touch on several key areas where we clearly see how much of an impact trauma has on the mind and brain to give you a big picture of what is happening.

Let's look at three parts of the brain bolded in this image: the prefrontal cortex (PFC), the hippocampus, and the amygdala.[4] The PFC is situated at the front of the brain just above the eyes, and it becomes very active when we self-regulate our thinking, feeling, and choosing. The hippocampus is situated behind the eyes in the middle of the brain, and it is connected with how we remember things as well as how we convert short-term memory into long-term memory. The amygdala is situated where the nose and eyes meet inside the brain, and it is like a library that sends information to the PFC, such as emotions and perceptions, so that we can judge danger and respond appropriately as well as practice better communication and empathy.

When someone has unmanaged trauma, the PFC starts slowing down and information gets distorted and warped, affecting decision-making and problem-solving.[5] This happens because the amygdala, instead of sending a steady stream of organized information to the PFC, sends information in a rapid-fire, erratic way. This is because a brain in a state of unmanaged trauma will continue to respond to the mind that is driving the brain function—if the mind is erratic and traumatized, the brain will respond as though it is still in danger.

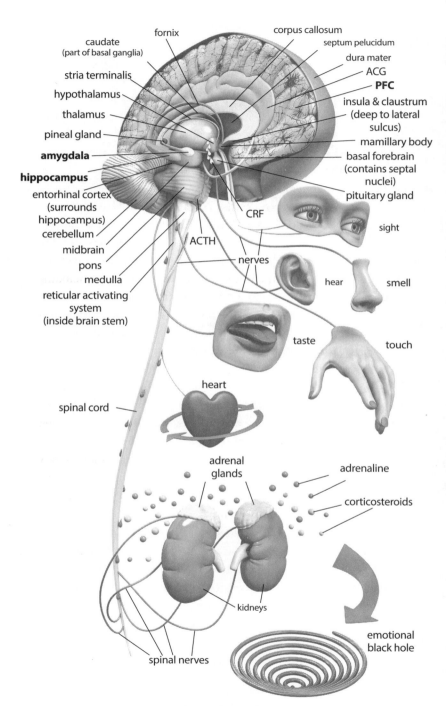

The neural networks

This unmanaged trauma disrupts the balance of different energy waves in the brain, which are generated by our thinking.[6] If our thinking is unmanaged, scary, overwhelming, and chaotic from a trauma, this will shape what waves flow through the brain, affecting its neurochemistry and electromagnetic activity by disrupting the balanced energy flow, bringing the brain out of its homeostatic, left-right brain balance range.

When this happens, things get messy. The PFC can't respond quickly enough to the amygdala, since the amygdala sends information to the PFC five times faster than the PFC sends back responses to the amygdala.[7] This will cause the hippocampus and the PFC to get smaller over time, which will affect memory and executive function. This, in turn, puts the rest of the body on high alert, including the adrenal glands, pituitary glands, hypothalamus, and HPA axis, which all respond by sending out lots of adrenaline, noradrenaline, epinephrine, cortisol, and glucose to try to make things better.

We observed this in our recent clinical trials. QEEG technology showed how unmanaged trauma and toxic thoughts showed up even when subjects closed their eyes—their brain stayed in a highly anxious active state.[8] Usually, when someone closes their eyes, the QEEG will capture a more reflective, intuitive state that looks like the rolling waves of the sea, but subjects with unmanaged trauma had waves reflecting something more like choppy zigzags. When people with a lot of unmanaged trauma and toxic thoughts close their eyes, their brain doesn't change frequencies like it should but stays in a highly active state for too long—this is called a high beta wave.[9] This state can be damaging over time because it tends to wear out healthy neural networks, like wearing out the tread on tires, and makes a person feel overwhelmed and acutely sensitized to what's happening so that they are easily triggered. This happens even more in a child's brain because their mind and neural circuits are still developing and maturing.

As this occurs, a child can start hearing or seeing things that aren't there, or not hearing or seeing things that are there. This state of mind can result in hypervigilance, hyperarousal, insomnia, nightmares, night sweats, flashbacks—overwhelming waves of emotion that just keep flowing—panic attacks, personality changes, becoming angry or aggressive easily, feeling increasingly anxious, feelings of detachment, and wanting to isolate because they feel they no longer fit into the world they're used to.[10] You may even notice that you or other family members may unwittingly become your child's "trigger." This can be very hard to understand as a parent or caregiver, which can result in feelings of guilt and shame—making the whole situation worse.

Additionally, if we don't deal with these traumas through mind-management, the conscious mind, brain, and body will start to wear out. This can eventually lead to physical symptoms such as hypertension, cardiovascular disease, GI issues, autoimmune issues, diabetes type 2, chronic fatigue syndrome, and so on.[11]

Trauma can also make a child feel different about who they are as a person. As mentioned above, trauma is carried in the nonconscious mind, brain, and body and manifests through the subconscious into the conscious mind as warning signals. Included in these warning signals are reactive coping patterns your child may have built into their neurology at the time of the traumatic incident, which have become reinforced over time.[12] These coping patterns can make your child feel frightened and vulnerable. Your child may start seeing nothing but threats and find it hard to imagine not suffering. This is why we need to help our children tune in to their four warning signals: emotions, behaviors, bodily sensations, and perspectives.

Brain-ee is reading lots of scary messages

This doesn't have to be your child's whole story. In our clinical trials, we also found that the eyes closed pattern seen on the QEEG headmaps changed from abnormally high active states to reflective and intuitive states once the subjects started using the Neurocycle.[13] So, as overwhelming as this may sound, you can help your child learn to regulate their brain activity and calm their mind and brain using the Neurocycle, thereby changing the structures of their mind and brain back to a healthier state.

Using the image of Brain-ee above, you can explain all this to your child. You can say something like, "Look at Brain-ee. He is reading a lot of scary stories out loud really fast, which makes him feel all scared and shaky and makes his body feel all muddled up! You may feel a lot like Brain-ee sometimes, and that's okay. But together we are going to change the story of the book so it doesn't make you feel so confused and scared, just like Brain-ee is going to change his story and make his thought trees better. We can do this using your Neurocycle superpower!"

15

Trauma and the Neurocycle

Whatever you do, don't despair. Our responses to trauma are perfectly reasonable in light of the experiences we have had—they are not brain diseases. They tell us that our mind, brain, and body are hard at work trying to help us adapt and cope.

In this chapter, you will see how to apply the Neurocycle to trauma. You can use the four warning signals table in chapter 3 and refer to part 2 to help you do the 5 Steps with your child. I also suggest that, as you work through the Neurocycle, you record your observations and your child's insights. This can look like the following:

Gather Awareness—Parent
Gather Awareness—Child
Reflect—Parent
Reflect—Child

And so on. You can write in the same or separate journals—whatever works for you and your child.

It's always a good idea to enlist the help of a therapist or mental health professional specializing in childhood trauma if you notice these signals are a consistent pattern in your child's life and are negatively impacting how they are managing school, relationships, homelife, and life in general. You and/or your child can do therapy alongside doing the Neurocycle daily.

Whatever you do, don't despair. Most children exposed to highly adverse or life-threatening events experience lingering short-term effects for a few days, weeks, or even months, including troubled dreams or nightmares and a sense of dread when reminded about the event. These responses are perfectly reasonable in light of the experiences they have had—they are not brain diseases. They tell us that their mind, brain, and body are hard at work trying to help them adapt and cope.

It's especially important with trauma to do some brain preparation before, after, and at any time during the Neurocycle as needed.

1. Gather Awareness

Below are a few examples of warning signals that you can look out for in children ages 3–10 (and older) that are potentially linked to trauma.

Some key *emotional* warning signals to look out for:

- Hovering anxiety (e.g., your child is shaking when they have to get ready for school or go somewhere)
- Depression (e.g., they seem persistently sad and listless and don't want to do anything)
- Panic (e.g., they freeze up, their eyes move rapidly from side to side, or they start crying and trying to get away when they have to do something or go somewhere)
- Fear (e.g., they are fearful at night and won't sleep without a light on or don't want to be alone)

Of course, sometimes these signals can show up but not be caused by trauma. However, if they are consistent and become disruptive to your child's daily life, they may be linked to a serious traumatic incident. The same goes for all the warning signal examples discussed below.

Some key *behavioral* warning signals to look out for:

- Reactions that seem out of proportion for the situation
- Hypervigilance (e.g., they are on high alert all the time, worried something is going to happen, or are very "wired")
- Hypovigilance (e.g., they are emotionally numb, almost as though their body and feelings are disconnected, and change from being outgoing to socially withdrawn and depressed)
- Overactivity (e.g., they need to keep busy all the time)
- Major behavior changes (e.g., they go from making good grades to failing, or they start cutting, which is directly related to control and the feeling of "at least I can control the pain")
- Hyperarousal (e.g., they are very jittery, get angry or worked up quickly, are startled by loud noises, or express inappropriate sexual behaviors)
- Sleep issues, including insomnia, nightmares, and night terrors
- Increased aggression (e.g., they hit you or a sibling, kick things, shout or scream, push other children, or say unkind things or words they shouldn't know at this age)
- Constant flashbacks
- Control issues
- Panic attacks
- Patterns of becoming aware of how they feel and then suppressing how they feel

- OCD-type symptoms
- Suicidal thoughts and attempts
- Learning problems
- Talking repeatedly about the event or pretending to "play" the event
- Tantrums or irritable outbursts
- Excessive clinging to caregivers and trouble separating
- Reverting to early behavior such as baby talk, bed-wetting, and thumb-sucking

Some key *bodily sensation* warning signals to look out for:

- Night sweats (e.g., they are sweating excessively and their pajamas are soaked)
- GI issues (e.g., they may complain frequently of an upset stomach, diarrhea, bloating, or lack of hunger)
- Unexplained pains (e.g., they may get ill frequently or complain that their heart is fluttering like a bird)

Some key *perspective* warning signals to look out for:

- Seem "flat" and without hope for the future or like they are depressed and are losing hope
- Believe lies about themselves, which impacts how they think, speak, and act (e.g., they shout at their doll and say things like, "You are a bad, bad doll! You are always wrong.")
- Seem to have a sense of dread, as though they are waiting for the absolute worst to happen
- Have very rigid boundaries as a way of feeling some control over their life
- Fear abandonment (e.g., they cry when you must leave them at day care or go out to do an errand)

- No longer like taking risks (e.g., when playing freely or playing with new friends, they are very wary and often don't join in the fun)

For Ages 3–5

To start the Gather Awareness step with your child age 3–5, show them the picture of Brain-ee walking through the forest in chapter 6 or use the Brain-ee toy (or any toy). Demonstrate, through playacting, Brain-ee walking up to a messy tree and say, "When Brain-ee looks at this tree, he sees there is a hurt in his brain. Brain-ee feels scared (emotional warning signal). This makes him shiver all over (bodily sensation warning signal) and want to hide (behavioral warning signal), so he doesn't want to play with anyone anymore (perspective warning signal). Do you want to show me what you think Brain-ee feels?" Then hand your child the Brain-ee toy or picture and let them playact. If they don't want to do this the first time, that's okay; you can demonstrate something you feel, and eventually they will join in.

General awareness of thought trees

For Ages 6–10

To start the Gather Awareness step with your child age 6–10, show them the picture of Brain-ee walking through the forest in chapter 6 and say, "Remember how we walked through the forest with Brain-ee earlier? And how there was that one tree that was big and messy? We need to pay attention to that tree because it needs help, and only you can fix it because this is your thought forest. But I can help you, so let's walk over to that tree and start looking at the branches—the warning signals—to see what we can do." You can then say something like, "So this tree represents the time your dad was very sick and passed away. This tree grew very strong because you were so sad and confused, and I was so sad and crying a lot. It was such an awful time, but Dad would want you to be happy again and remember all the good times with him. So, let's see how we can mend the roots to grow all the happy memories and make them bigger and stronger than the sad memories on the tree. It's okay if sometimes you want to look at the sad memories and cry and maybe even feel angry that Daddy isn't here to see all the wonderful things you are doing. But to help you manage each day and get stronger, we need more of the healthy memories like in this picture of Brain-ee."

Brain-ee enjoying his healthy thought tree development

2. Reflect

The Reflect step helps your child identify the altered and distorted way they may see their self and their life after extreme trauma. In this step, you want to help your child focus more deeply on the warning signals from Step 1. Your goal here is to help your child see what thought tree the warning signals are pointing to.

As you work through this step, remember that a young child is able to be introspective but does not yet have the metacognitive and linguistic skills to verbalize their thoughts. This is why it is important to have toys, paper and coloring pens, or art materials available if possible when doing the Neurocycle with your child to help them express what they feel. You can even use packets and boxes and do the step in your kitchen, another room in your home, or your garden—be creative and flexible.

For Ages 3–5

Give your child age 3–5 the Brain-ee toy or other toys to answer the questions or let them draw the answers. You can even draw for them or with them as you prompt them with questions. It's great to let a child this age distance themselves from their warning signals by transferring how they feel to a doll, toy, or drawing.

Brain-ee has a sore tummy

For example:

> "I see your doll is very sad. Why is it sad? Can you show me?"
>
> "Your doll has a very upset tummy today, and their legs are all tingly. Do you know why?"
>
> "I see your doll is very jumpy and talking a lot. I wonder why. Can you help me understand?"

Brain-ee feels jumpy and is talking a lot

For Ages 6–10

You can work through this step with your child age 6–10 by helping them put their signals into full sentences. You can construct a variety of sentences for your child, as they may not have all the words they need at this age to describe how they feel.

Always make sure you reassure them that they are wonderful and special as you do this. Remind them that they are not "bad" if they have an ugly thought tree in their head because we all have them, and we all need to do this work to make our trees better. Also remind them that something happened to make the thought tree grow there, and you are here to help them find out what it was. You can also show them the thought trees and Brain-ee pictures in part 2 to help you explain this.

For example:

> "I see you feel sad a lot lately. Maybe someone hurt you or said something to you or did something to you? You did

nothing wrong. Would you like to describe to me what is on the tree?"

"I can give you some words to choose from, and you can tell me which one you feel the most. Or we can use pictures for you to show me."

"Let's work out where it feels sore in your body, and maybe we can look at what you are saying and doing and see how these are all tied to what happened."

3. Write/Play/Draw

As you do the Gather Awareness and Reflect steps with your child, make sure you keep a journal record of your observations, as mentioned above. This will be helpful if you go to a therapist, if you need to explain something to family and friends when necessary, or if any potential legal recourse is needed.

For Ages 3–5

Your child age 3–5 can use toys; playact; or use drawings, art, or cut-out pictures to express how they feel. You can use the boxes explained in part 2 for this. You may have to do some of the writing or drawing with them to help them, and you may have to do more prompting with words, phrases, and questions than for older children.

For Ages 6–10

Encourage your child age 6–10 to write however they want to. They can use drawings, art, or cut-out pictures; write words in a journal; or simply use toys or playact. Help them understand that healing is a long journey. Keep a journal of what happens so you can both look back at your child's accomplishments and see the progress they are making. It's hard work, but it's worth it!

4. Recheck

It's really important with trauma that you don't stop at the Write/Play/Draw step but help your child find ways to "mend the branches that are broken." This is a "How do we mend this?" step, as I spoke about in depth in part 2. Always use the Recheck question as a guide: *This has happened. Now, what can we do to manage this?* Remind your child that the story doesn't just go away. Rather, you will help them learn how to manage the story.

When I spoke to Tim about this, he explained what the Recheck for him was all about: "I don't accept a problem without a solution." You can use this description to help your child understand what they need to do in this step.

For Ages 3–5

If your child age 3–5 drew a picture of the situation in the Write/Play/Draw step, you can ask them if they can redraw the picture to show what they would rather see happen (reconceptualization). You can even prompt them and help them draw a new picture or find new words to explain the old picture. Once again, you can use the boxes of pictures from part 2. You can also narrate while they are drawing to help them explain what they are doing and encourage them to nod yes or shake no to guide what you are saying. In this way, they get the words to express the changes they want. You can also do this if your child acted out Step 3.

Here are a few other Recheck tips to help your child reconceptualize traumatic events:

- "The terrible story is behind you. Let's draw a new picture and make a new story together."
- "You're changing your brain because you have a superpower, and that means you will feel much better, just like superhero Brain-ee!"

"Let's make a list of or draw all the things that are already better."

For Ages 6–10

For older children, this step can be done via words, sentences, pictures, or all three. Older children may want to point out their own prompts.

Here are a few other Recheck tips to help your child reconceptualize traumatic events:

"You don't have to be scared anymore, because this is no longer a secret. I'm here to help you."

"It's okay to feel sad now and then, because what happened to make you sad won't go away—you'll still remember it. But it's good to have a plan so you don't think about it for too long and have a happy memory to think about when you remember the sad memory." (Show and discuss the image of Brain-ee enjoying his healthy thought tree development in Step 1 above.)

"Look at this picture [show a picture of something that is broken]. It shows everything broken. Now, let's draw the picture again with the broken bits mended in a beautiful way. We could even make a beautiful new picture!" (This is a good place to use the kintsugi principle activity I spoke about in part 2, where you use gold, glitter, or other beautiful paint or glue to put something broken back together in Step 4.)

"Let's find different solutions so that you don't have to feel like this anymore."

Answer your child's questions about their experiences. They may be shocking for you to hear. These are a sign that they are tuning in to their nonconscious mind, and this is a good thing. Answer briefly but honestly, in a way they can understand. When your child brings something up, first ask for clarification so you can understand exactly what their concern is. Usually, children ask a question because they are worried about something specific. Give a reassuring answer. If you don't know an answer to a question, it's okay to say, "I don't know. We can try to find out." Try not to speculate or repeat rumors in front of your child.

Below is Tim's Neurocycle Recheck sheet on "fear." He fills it in and then chooses his favorite statement for the day to use as his Active Reach, writing it at the bottom of the sheet. He sees this Neurocycle as an Active Reach generator. He also wears a watch that reminds him, through seven daily alarms, when to practice his Active Reach. You can do something similar with your child if you wish.

5. Active Reach

With severe trauma, it's very important that you work on *simple* Active Reaches each day with your child. Take something that

I don't like feeling scared. Here are some fears that I wish didn't happen and want to change:

•
•
•
•
•
•

Draw a picture changing your fear into a happy truth. You can choose any ending!

I can change my fear because feelings are just opinions. I do not need to be afraid because I have:
I can fight my fear with this fact/truth:

Tim's Neurocycle sheet on fear

really stood out to them when doing the Recheck step and turn this into a simple statement with a visualization. Set a reminder to practice this Active Reach at least seven times during the day, as discussed in part 2. Let your child know that as they do this, they are making their thought tree stronger and healthier.

For Ages 3–5

Here are several ideas for your child's Active Reach:

- Make your child feel safe with extra cuddling, hugs, or a reassuring pat on the back throughout the day. This will help them feel secure and safe, which is important in the aftermath of a frightening or disturbing experience.
- Say to your child, "Every time you feel sad and your body gets sore, think of the nice, new picture you drew."
- Let them pick out an item of clothing, such as a hat, and tell them to put it on themselves or a toy to remind them they are safe. Or you can hold a picture they like that they can look at as a reminder that they are safe.
- Suggest that they can hug themselves, give themselves a high five in the mirror, or smile at themselves in the mirror when they feel bad.
- Encourage them to write "I am . . ." statements on a pretty piece of paper decorated with a heart or star or whatever stickers they have (e.g., "I am confident, I am happy, I am kind, I am brave, I am patient, I am loved, I am a good friend, I am proud of myself, I am safe, I am awesome").
- Give them activities to do as a healthy distraction and mood shifter, such as building with blocks or helping bake and decorate cookies.
- Use the Brain-ee affirmation pages in the Brain-ee coloring book if you have it.

For Ages 6–10

Children ages 6–10 are often comforted by facts; knowledge is very empowering and helps relieve anxiety. Here are some suggestions to help you make Active Reaches that will help them practice their newly reconceptualized thought tree:

- Use simple images, such as, "This was a hurricane in your life, but the hurricane has passed, and now we are cleaning up the debris." You can use whatever imagery works.
- Make Active Reaches that are knowledge-based about the trauma; for example, "That person said terrible things to you that weren't true, but they felt true. You are learning to wire this out of your brain and make the thought tree healthy."
- Help them make hopeful Active Reaches about the future. Children this age need to see the future to help them recover. They value specifics. For example, in the event of a war or natural disaster, you can say, "People from all over the country and world are sending all kinds of help, like food and doctors, and helping to build new homes. It won't always be like this!"

Additional Tips for Helping Your Child through Trauma

Below are some additional tips you may find helpful as you work through the Neurocycle with your child to overcome a past trauma. These also make great Active Reach prompts.

- Try to avoid saying things like, "Time heals all wounds," which can come across as dismissive of the emotions your child feels in *that* moment. It isn't that statements like this are not true, but in the moments your child is expressing their emotions, it may not feel true or real for them and can be counterproductive. For example, if your family has experienced loss and you and your child are grieving, those moments of intense pain are not "okay"—the key thing to communicate to your child is that it is okay to not be okay. It's better to say things like, "Nothing feels good right now, but we will sit through these feelings together. I see your pain, and I will support you and hold your hand in these moments when this is all you feel." By doing so, you create a space where your child knows they are safe to express *any* emotion they have and will be supported.

- Try to avoid saying, "I understand exactly how you feel," because we can never fully understand an experience someone else has. You may have been through similar trauma, but the way you see and understand the trauma in your life will be different from how your child sees and understands their trauma.

- It's perfectly okay for children to have happy and sad stories. As parents or caregivers, we often want to shield our children from the bad side of life, but this is impossible. Remind yourself that part of your job is to help your child manage their sad stories, not to stop them from thinking about them or to eradicate them.

- In the immediate aftermath of trauma, the first things we need to do are offer our children support, provide decompression techniques, and meet their basic needs, such as physical and emotional comfort. Focusing immediately on trying to get your child to express all their feelings and talk about what has happened to them can backfire. Their neurophysiology is in a state of shock; the mind, brain, and body are not in a rational state. If you try to solve everything at once, chances are the situation will get worse, because your child's heightened state of mind will affect how they process what happened, wiring the unhealthy trauma thought tree more deeply into the brain and body.

16

■■■■■■■■

Identity Issues

When a child loses their sense of self, it can result in feelings of bitterness, rage, anxiety, worry, self-pity, envy, pride, jealousy, cynicism, hopelessness, and depression. This isn't just a child being naughty or difficult—they are going through an identity crisis.

The traumas and challenges of life tend to build a huge block around our identity—who we are at our core and how we shape our identity over time. Trying to discover who we are can feel like an endless and even pointless task. However, even though this is hard, takes time, and often takes more than a little help, it is doable. This is a task we need to teach our children from a young age onward.

An Identity Story

I want to share a story I heard years ago. Day after day, a little boy sat on a wall watching a man chip away at a huge block of marble. Fascinated, he finally built up enough courage to ask the man why he was doing this—a task that seemed to be going nowhere. The man replied, "I am chipping away at this block because inside there is an angel waiting to come out." This man was the prodigious artist Michelangelo, and the angel was his famous statue of David. (This story has been attributed to Michelangelo, although its exact origin is unknown.)

Teaching our children to find and shape their identity can feel a lot like this—long and arduous. Yet when we give them the tools to discover their own "David," we can help them make their story into a work of art, something beautiful and unique to them.

We each have a unique way of thinking, feeling, and choosing that produces our singular thoughts and experiences and gives us a sense of value and self-worth. I call this our customized thinking or "I-factor." It is the unique way our mind-in-action (discussed in part 1) works through our brain, producing our unique identity.

Even though we all have the same brain parts and neurophysiology, different parts of the brain will be activated and grow in different ways as we uniquely think, feel, and choose in response to life.[1] This results in diversity in the resultant growth of dendrites on the neurons, where memories are stored (see images in chapter 1). It's almost as though our brain tissue, right down to the level of particles and subatomic particles, is arranged in a particular manner matching our customized ability to digest and process information from our experiences.

The way each of us thinks is powerful and different from but complementary to everyone else's thinking, feeling, and choosing. As we think, we create customized realities, and as we operate in these exclusive realities, everyone benefits because we offer the world something no one else can.

Nature, Nurture, I-Factor

The framework for our customized thinking and identity is laid down in our genes (nature), influenced by our upbringing (nurture), and *activated* by our I-factor. This triad results in a unique worldview, belief system, way of communication, and behavior.

Our I-factor is incredibly important; it has what I call "veto power." It can override our nurture and develop our nature, which opens us up to all kinds of possibilities. We can learn, with our mind, to recognize when our I-factor is "offline" and bring it back again after a traumatic or challenging experience. We can learn to restore *and* continue to grow our identity.

This is a skill we need to teach our children from a young age, because we cannot protect them from all the elements of life. Children, when functioning in their customized way of thinking, feeling, and choosing, operate in and shape their unique identity even when they struggle, which helps them harness their inspiration, creativity, excitement, peace, kindness, and joy. They tend to be more self-regulated, compassionate, and calm and have a feeling of purpose and direction.

However, if nurture is left unchecked and unmanaged, it can shape how your child shows up and grows up. Surrounding belief systems, religious views, people's expectations, social media, cultural dictates, and toxic relationships and influences all can affect your child's customized thinking, which can have a downstream effect on their self-worth and identity.[2]

Loss of the Sense of Self

When a child loses their sense of self, it can result in feelings of bitterness, rage, anxiety, worry, self-pity, envy, pride, jealousy, cynicism, hopelessness, and depression.[3] This isn't just a child being naughty or difficult—they are going through an identity crisis. These feelings are warning signals that are letting them know that something is wrong and disrupting their thinking.

We saw this play out in all areas of Tim's life (see chapter 14). Weekly, his parents were called into his school for issues such as his lack of focus, disruptive verbal behaviors, aggression with other children, defiance, refusal to complete his work, and inability to comply with regular commands and rules. At home, Tim struggled to follow directions, remember basic daily tasks, and emotionally adjust to extracurricular activities with other kids. Socially, this left him without friends and struggling to find a place where he felt understood or like he belonged, which is why his parents eventually decided to homeschool him.

An identity crisis at its heart is an existential crisis. It's something we must recognize in our children, validate, and help them manage, because it cuts to the core of their being and will impact what they think and how they behave, their self-esteem and who they become, and how they love themselves.[4]

If left unmanaged, an identity crisis can lead to a sense of shame that can easily creep into all aspects of a child's life, leading to major mental health issues and even suicidal ideation.[5] We need to remind ourselves constantly that our children are behaving like this *because* of something. This is not who they are but who they have become because of what has happened to them, which is affecting their customized way of thinking, feeling, and choosing. If we can step in and help them regulate their toxic thoughts and memories, which manifest in painful emotions, behaviors, bodily sensations, and perspectives—the warning signals—we can stop these signals from evolving into depressive episodes, prolonged anxiety, panic attacks, psychotic episodes, and suicidal ideation.

Our Unique Customized Thinking Is Reflected in the Mind and Brain

As mentioned above, the unique customized way of thinking, feeling, and choosing that is expressed in the identity of a person is also reflected in the structure of their brain. As neuroscientists Peter Sterling and Simon Laughlin note in their book *Principles of Neural Design*, everyone has their own unique manifestation of two hundred specialized areas in the cortex of the brain that are made up of many specialized circuits—this is the basis of each person's unique identity.[6] These unique patterns enable each of us to make our own unique contribution to the world. These specializations partly explain why some individuals are born with innate talents, like Mozart—he came out of the womb with that "special something" in him. This means your child also came out of the womb with a "special something." They have something to give to the world that no one else can!

However, when your child's identity is threatened, their customized thinking, feeling, and choosing—their mind-in-action—becomes derailed, and this shows up in the brain as an imbalance or lack of coherence between the two sides of the brain, which will impact their cognitive reasoning and flexibility, which, in turn, will impact their sense of self. The brain is very sensitive to the mind, and this can be seen in the waves of the brain—delta, theta, alpha, beta, and gamma—and in the relationships between these frequencies as well as in how blood and different neurochemicals flow in the brain.[7]

So, for example, when someone is going through an identity crisis, this can be reflected in the brain as low energy activity in the frontal lobe and pockets of high beta energy across the temporal lobe. Theta energy can also decrease in the frontal lobe, creating alpha and beta asymmetry, and as the amplitude of high beta increases, gamma tends to decrease.[8] All this collectively can reduce blood flow, and with less blood flow and oxygen, the ability to think clearly or rationally will plummet.[9] Proteins misfold inside the thoughts, and there is electrochemical chaos, which activates a protective immune response.[10] If the issue setting all this off in the first place is not dealt with, then this response can become a hyperimmune response,[11] which can lead to more damage in the brain and body, increasing your child's vulnerability to disease because of increased cortisol and homocysteine levels.[12] Even the telomeres on chromosomes can become damaged.[13]

Consequently, your child's ability to self-regulate drops, which reduces their ability to tap into their intuition and monitor how they are thinking about and speaking to themselves. They may become less kind to themselves, and their sense of self-value will decrease; their mind has become overwhelmed with the "noise" of harsh, unmanaged, and intrusive thoughts. This can result in behaviors such as self-loathing, low self-esteem, self-sabotaging, parent-pleasing, shock-absorbing, toxic shame, and increased sensitivity.

For example, your child may spend a lot of time on social media. This can be beneficial in some ways, such as connecting with friends and family or learning more about a topic they are interested in. However, this can also have detrimental effects on their identity if it results in a toxic cycle of comparison, making your child feel insecure in their own life because of what they see other people doing.[14] They may start thinking that there is something intrinsically lacking or wrong with them, which may result in behavior changes, including increased aggression, people-pleasing, an eating disorder, acting depressed, or social anxiety.

Boundaries and Identity

Teaching your child about boundaries is very important in helping them manage their identity, much in the same way that teaching your child about boundaries with other people helps them understand relationships and their community better. Boundaries allow children to explore who they are in a safe way.

One great way to teach your child about boundaries is by giving them different options for events that happen daily and allowing your child to choose. For example, when your child wants to play with something that may not be safe for them, and you ask them not to play with it because it may hurt them, give them several other options and let them decide what they want to play with. In this case, you set a boundary, explained why, and then let them choose what they wanted to do instead, which helped them feel empowered in a moment that had the potential to impact their developing sense of autonomy and self-identity.[15]

Whenever you as a parent or caregiver set a boundary, also make sure that you explain why. Just saying something like "Because I said so" tends to link fear to punishment and can teach children that overriding another person's questions is okay if they think they are wiser than the other person, which isn't a healthy habit to encourage.[16] I know this is hard for many of us because, yes, in many ways we are smarter than our children, and we have experienced more life. However, this does not mean your child isn't their own person—someone who is growing and learning about the world—and they should be encouraged to ask questions. In fact, when you tell your child to do something and they ask why, this is one of the best opportunities for a teaching moment that will help your child better explore and understand their self and their place in the world. Remember, we are only experts in our own experiences.

> **Whenever you as a parent or caregiver set a boundary, also make sure that you explain why.**

When you set limits or boundaries to protect yourself and your child, try to use language that doesn't just shut your child down. For example, if your child demands your attention but you are busy in a meeting or on a phone call, try not to just push them away and tell them to stop bothering you. Let them know before the call that you will play with them or cuddle them after you are done. In this way, you let them know that you will take care of their needs but need to address your own first, which is a perfect example of boundaries: setting your own individual limits but also showing a willingness to take care of the needs of people you love.

Many times, parents feel overworked and burned out, and this often stems from the fact that they haven't been setting boundaries with their children. This can be really hard as a parent. It is difficult to see the line between raising your child and attending to their needs and overfunctioning and wearing yourself out. I recommend doing your own Neurocycle to work out what boundaries you need to function as a parent or caregiver so that you can show up for your child in a way that enhances your relationship and helps your child grow as a person.

One of the most important things to remember about setting boundaries with your child is that you can simultaneously set boundaries while respecting and validating the other person's experience and emotions. We must respect our children's space, time, privacy, and emotions, even when they are really young, just as we want to teach them how to respect our space, time, privacy, and emotions. If we want our children to learn how to set healthy boundaries with other people, they need to "practice" by setting boundaries with the people they feel very safe with—us. This is why it is so important to practice tuning in to your child and listening to what they do and don't feel okay with.

I understand that this can be hard to do, so take it one day at a time. There are many times when we need to enforce our will on our children for their own learning and growth—such as making children brush their teeth, put on their shoes, or wash their hands.

However, sometimes the necessary parts of parenting can override a child's will in ways that are unnecessary. There are times it is better to try to teach our children about boundaries by respecting their own limitations and boundaries. For example, some young children may not like too much physical touch even from their own parents, and that is fine! As parents, we need to respect their physical space boundaries as they figure out what they need in the moment, even when it is hard for us to understand exactly what is happening. The key thing is to be there for your child and let them know they can come to you if they have an issue. Creating a space for your child to feel like they can explore who they are and what they want is paramount.[17]

Even though children may not fully grasp the concept of boundaries, they are very aware that there are certain things they do not enjoy—which may change over time. When you respect your child's space and let them know that you want them to explore who they are and what they want, you are helping instill confidence in them and letting them know it's okay to express their needs or boundaries.[18] This also teaches children from a young age that saying no is okay, which will help them learn the value of consent.

A great way to explain this to your child is by thinking out loud about what you would say to someone who yells at you or says nasty things. How would you tell this person that you can't engage with them? Work through an example like this with your child, and then explain to them that setting boundaries with their thoughts is similar, except that they do this with their negative thoughts instead of with another person. For example, when Tim found himself saying things to himself like *I am difficult*, he would change this to *No, you are not difficult. You have been through difficult stuff from people who were supposed to love you. They are the difficult ones.*

An Unmanaged Identity Crisis Can Have Pervasive Effects

Recent research demonstrates that a child's sense of self is developed as young as four and potentially even younger.[19] The idea that young children think about themselves only in concrete ways and, unlike adults or older children, aren't able to reason about their traits or their self-worth and identity as individuals is incorrect. As mentioned earlier, children are a lot more insightful than previous research has shown. This means that their identity is more malleable and more impacted by what they experience than we used to understand or believe.

The identities of young children are being shaped by everything and everyone around them. This means that they are not exclusively focused on concrete behaviors and results, such as *I painted a nice picture* but are capable of thinking about themselves in terms of general traits and abilities, such as *I can paint well.* They are also able to form an opinion and have insight into their worth as individuals based on what they experience, such as *I am a good boy because I do and say* _____.[20] However, it is important to remember that just as children can understand and think positively about themselves, they can also think negatively and become dispirited when they struggle or feel they have failed.[21]

The implications of this research are twofold. First, children are able to understand and reason with their emotions at a young age, which means that we *need* to proactively and continually help our children process what is happening in their life in order to preserve and grow their identity. Second, if we do not proactively help our children process and manage their life experiences, as well as their insight and reasoning, their identity can be affected. We need to constantly remind ourselves that a child's insight about their self is dependent on and shaped by the people in their life *and* their limited life experience.

When we use "you are" statements, our children may reason themselves into thinking that this is the only way they can act and make it a part of how they self-identify.

The ability of young children to reason flexibly about their abilities and their sense of self-worth and identity is contextually driven. This means it is impacted by their experiences—the memories inside thoughts—*and* the people in their life. As a result, we need to be very careful with the words we choose to describe our children's behaviors, specifically when using "you are" statements. The words and statements we choose can direct our children down the wrong path because our children generally believe what we say to them.[22]

When we use "you are" statements, our children may reason themselves into thinking that this is the only way they *can* act and make it a part of how they self-identify. So, instead of seeing stubbornness or aggressiveness as a behavioral reaction to a situation, for example, your child may instead think it is part of who they are—something they cannot escape. Additionally, when they receive negative reinforcement for these behaviors, they may reason that *I am bad and cannot help myself. My parents are saying this to me, and they are angry and blaming me or punishing me, so I must be bad.*

This is why we need to choose our words very carefully and make sure we aren't defining our children by or with negativity. Rather, we need to show them that the way they are acting now does not define who they are forever. Instead of saying "You are so difficult" if your child doesn't want to put their shoes on, you can say something like, "I see you don't want to put your shoes on. This isn't because you are naughty, so there must be a reason. Can you help me understand why?" Wording how you respond in this way appeals to your child's cognitive reasoning and gives them a chance to develop their mental flexibility and build their identity in a constructive way.

"You are" statements break a child's identity down, but "You are behaving like this for a reason" statements build healthy, flexible reasoning that enhances and doesn't attack your child's developing sense of identity. It encourages them to view themselves from another perspective, which is great for their mental growth and resilience. It tells them, "It's okay. I know this is not the real you. Let's work out, together, why you feel this way." This builds up your child's sense of autonomy and empowerment, which is a crucial aspect of identity development.

Safety Net Parenting versus Helicopter Parenting

To help our children develop this sense of autonomy and build identity, we as parents and caregivers need to know how to get involved in our children's lives without smothering them. "Helicopter parenting" is taking an overprotective or excessive interest in the life of your child. It's the kind of parenting that constantly shadows a child, directing their every movement and filling their every moment. It does not give them enough alone time to play or grow freely; helicopter parenting takes away opportunities for a child to learn and develop healthy life skills and habits.[23]

This kind of parenting impacts a child's mental growth, sending the message *My parents don't trust me to do this on my own, so there must be something wrong with or lacking in me.* This can affect their self-esteem, especially if the parent or caregiver is always there to clean up their mess instead of teaching the child that "It's okay to make a mistake, and here's how you can make things better." The child will never learn how to cope with loss, disappointment, or failure, which impacts their mental development as they age.[24] Many studies have found that helicopter parenting can make children feel less competent when dealing with and managing the stresses of life on their own. It has been associated with higher levels of anxiety and depression in children, which can get worse as they progress into adulthood unless managed.[25]

There are many reasons parents adopt this style of care, including a fear of the future or the world or the need to protect children from harms they may have experienced growing up. In many cases, adults who felt unloved, neglected, or ignored as children may overcompensate with their own children. However, these insecurities will be picked up by the child, and they will then need to try to use their limited experience to interpret these signals. Unfortunately, their default may be to blame themselves in some way because of their desire to please their parent, which will, in turn, affect their sense of self as they grow.[26]

It is far better to adopt a "safety net parenting" style. This kind of parenting makes a space for a child to struggle, allows them to be disappointed and upset, and then helps them to work through their feelings safely without judgment.[27] It teaches the child to have a mindset that learns and grows and isn't afraid of failure. It is defined by a sense of *This is what doesn't work, and that's okay. Let's repair, learn, and grow.* This kind of parenting looks for opportunities to let children do what they're physically and mentally capable of doing—to step back but still stay in the room. It helps a child build up their own value and resilience, which will, in turn, help them shape their own identity.

To understand this style of parenting, imagine your child is learning to be an acrobat. You nervously watch them climb to the top of the ladder, slipping periodically on the rungs. Then you watch as they stand on the tiny ledge—they are about to launch themselves onto a swing or walk on a tightrope. See yourself as the safety net below; you have your arms open wide to catch your child if they fall, but only after they have struggled and tried. You are there to save them from dejection and to bounce them back up again so they can try once more. You are the foundation that gives them the courage to keep going—to practice walking that tightrope, swinging through the air, or performing spectacular gymnastic feats.

Removing all challenges and overindulging a child will make them feel frustrated and entitled, which will stunt their mental development and growth. On the other hand, when you teach them to embrace the challenges they face and process and reconceptualize what they are going through, you help them develop their character and find the greatness that is within them—their unique gift to the world.

17

■■■■■■■■

Identity Issues and the Neurocycle

It's easy and common for anyone, including children, to slip in and out of how they understand themselves. The key is to help your child have a mental plan in place for when they do experience moments of self-crisis so that these feelings don't take over and consume their sense of self.

Remember, as you work through an identity Neurocycle with your child, I recommend recording your observations and insights in a journal.

For ages 3–5: a young child generally sees who they are by how others perceive them; you are like a mirror to them.[1] Children start taking this "reflection" into themselves and incorporating it into their identity from a young age, which is why I recommend using the Neurocycle first yourself before reacting to your child so that you can become more aware of and manage what you reflect back to your child. As a parent of four myself, I know firsthand how easy it is to get worked up and reactive, to say or do something you will later regret. We all need a little help sometimes.

For ages 6–10: older children tend to value their peer group more, and this will impact how they view themselves.[2] Peer connection is very important to them. At this time in their life, we need to make sure that we don't compare our children to their peers, siblings, friends, or cousins, as this can have a negative impact on how they see themselves. Children in this age group also need to have many open conversations, which will help them learn how to use words and phrases to describe who they are, what they like and don't like, what they believe, their favorite activities, and so on.

1. Gather Awareness

With your child, use the Brain-ee character to prompt them and ask questions as they Gather Awareness of their warning signals.
Here are some suggestions on how to do this:

- Observe your child. Are they expressing emotional warning signals as a pattern, such as constant anger, anxiety, worry, self-pity, envy, pride, jealousy, cynicism, or hopelessness? To what extent? How long has this been going on?
- How have their behaviors changed? To what extent and for how long?
- Gather Awareness of any associated bodily sensation warning signals that your child is experiencing, such as headaches, heart palpitations, or GI issues. To what extent? How long has this pattern been going on?
- What is their attitude toward themselves like? How do they see themselves?

Use these prompts to shape your questions and help your child Gather Awareness of how they feel about themselves.

For Ages 3–5

- Using their emotional warning signal box (see part 2), ask your child to take out a picture showing how they feel about themselves; for example, this could be a picture of someone making angry faces at themselves in the mirror.
- Using their behavioral warning signal box, ask your child to take out a picture showing what they are doing that indicates they are mad at themselves; for example, this could be a picture of a person shouting at other people.
- Using their bodily sensation warning signal box, ask your child to take out a picture showing where they are hurting in their body. This could be a picture of someone with a headache.
- Using their perspective warning signal box, ask your child to take out which pair of sunglasses they feel best represents how they feel about themselves right now.

For Ages 6–10

- Using their emotional warning signal box, ask your child to take out a picture, word, or phrase that best explains how they are feeling about themselves.
- Using their behavioral warning signal box, ask your child to take out a picture, word, or phrase that best explains what they are doing that shows how they feel about themselves.
- Using their bodily sensation warning signal box, ask your child to take out a picture, word, or phrase that best explains how the way they feel about themselves feels in their body.
- Using their perspective warning signal box, ask your child to take out a picture, word, or phrase that best explains their attitude toward their friends, school, siblings, life in general, and so on.

2. Reflect

Below are some prompts as you do Step 2 of the Neurocycle with your child to understand how they perceive themselves and their worth.

- Is there a pattern to these warning signals?
- When did they start?
- How long have they been going on?
- Can your child associate any specific changes in their life to when these patterns started showing up?
- Does your child seem like they feel ashamed of themselves or bad about themselves? Why?
- Does your child seem to be struggling to find a sense of meaning and passion?
- What do you think has happened in their life (what's the story) to affect their identity?

For Ages 3–5

You can ask your child:

"If your toys could talk, what would they say about you?"

"What does it feel like when I hug you?"

"Can you draw what is in your head right now?"

"What do you think you're going to dream about tonight?"

"What do you like best (sounds, games, people, foods, activities, and so on)? Why?"

For Ages 6–10

You can ask your child:

"Are you struggling to discover what you love?"

"What do you think has happened in your life to affect how you see yourself?"

"I see you seem less motivated and excited about life, school, and friendships lately. Why do you think you feel this way? Can I help in any way?"

"What's going on that's making you feel bad about yourself?"

"Think about all the things you like to do and are good at. Can you list those things? If not, why?" (Try to see whether they struggle to answer or don't have an answer anymore.)

"Why do you think this is happening?"

"Why do you want to be like that other person?"

3. Write/Play/Draw

As you do the Gather Awareness and Reflect steps with your child, make sure you keep a journal record of your observations, as mentioned above. This will be helpful if you go to a therapist, if you need to explain something to family and friends, or if you need to help organize your own thinking so that you can better understand what your child is going through and how you can help them. Below are some prompts as you do Step 3 of the Neurocycle with your child to capture and develop more insights into how they perceive themselves and their worth.

For Ages 3–5

Let your child draw, act, or use pictures related to what you Gathered Awareness of and Reflected on to organize their thinking and find out more about how they feel. You can help them do this by taking each of the pictures or words they took out of the warning signal boxes in Step 1 and sticking them into a journal. Then you can help your child add more pictures or words as they think of more things connected to how they feel. You can also ask your child if they want to act this out with their toys.

Let your child guide you and tell you how much help they need. Remember to practice safety net parenting—it can be very tempting to jump in before your child asks for help, so try to resist this impulse. Your child doesn't have to play, write, or draw a lot in each session. You will have lots of time to help them learn how to manage and build their identity, so try not to rush the process.

For Ages 6–10

Let your child put the pictures, words, or phrases they took from the warning signal boxes in a journal and then ask them to write a sentence about each one. They can also add or draw pictures alongside these if they want. Encourage your child to write or draw anything that comes into their mind regarding how they think about themselves. Give them as much or as little help as they want. Let them guide you.

4. Recheck

In Step 4, work out a few ways you think will help your child see themselves differently and try to find an example from your own life to help you explain. This is a great way to connect with your child and will help them realize you have also battled with how you see yourself. This will help them see that these kinds of struggles are a normal part of being a human.

As you work through this step, remember the discussion in the last chapter about "You are" statements and how they can break a child's identity down. Focus on "You are behaving like this for a reason" statements instead, which help build flexible reasoning and encourage your child to view themselves from another perspective.

Don't forget to write down or draw whatever you discuss and reconceptualize with your child in the Recheck step. This is a collaborative effort between you and your child, so you can write what you feel is important, and your child can help with words, phrases, and/or drawings.

For Ages 3–5

- Help your child look closer at what they discovered in Steps 1–3 to see if there are any underlying patterns so they can reconceptualize the thought tree that is shaping what they are thinking, saying, and doing. For example, you can say something like this to your child: "I can see you get mad if your brother doesn't let you be the boss of the game. How about we let your brother play the game his way first and then you show him how you want to play it your way?" By doing this, you help your child notice that they are driven by a desire for efficiency and effectiveness, and their strength could be in their incredible ability to organize games or projects. They just need to work out better ways to do this instead of getting mad, which you can help them do.

- You can help them better understand why there is a boundary. For example, you can say, "I can see that it makes you upset to wait until I'm finished with what I am doing, and I'm sorry that you are upset, but it is important that I get my stuff done. Is there something you can do while you wait for me?" Help them turn their frustration into a constructive activity that makes them happy and taps into their identity (e.g., something they love to do). You can also say something like, "I can see you're bummed that I want to watch my show for a bit, but I need to do certain things that make me happy, just like it is important for you to do things that make you happy. What would you like to do while I am busy?" This will help them see that you are different from them but also need to do things that are important to you and help you feel more like "you," just as certain things make them feel more like who they are. Or you might say, "I can see that you are mad because I turned off the TV, and I want you to feel safe expressing those feelings to me, but it is bedtime. You might be very tired if you don't get enough sleep." Every child has a social identity, which is how they perceive their various roles in society in relation to others. Children derive a sense of pride, self-worth, and consistency from their social identities, so it's important to encourage them to do this type of boundary rechecking.

For Ages 6–10

With your child age 6–10, you can ask them if they would like to answer the Recheck questions on their own or if they want you to help them. Tell them something like, "I know you will be very good at finding the answers to these questions. I will help only if you need me to."

For example, you can say things like:

"It's okay; being angry [or however they feel] is not the real you. Let's work out why you feel this way together."

"I notice sometimes that you find yourself feeling a lot of jealousy [or whatever emotion they have] in situations like this. When you feel this way, you can ask yourself questions like *What exactly am I jealous of? Why? What can I learn from that person I'm jealous of? Why did this particular friend or situation make me feel jealous? What can I do about this? What am I proud of and want to see myself doing more of?* I do this all the time when I feel jealous, and it really helps me!"

"How about instead of comparing yourself to those people, you ask yourself why you want to or why you feel the need to compare yourself to them?"

As you work through this step with your child, you may find it helpful to teach them to start identifying flaws and common mistakes they may be making that are part of their identity crisis.

Emphasize that it isn't a shaming exercise; rather, they are getting to know themselves better, and this will help them. You can explain to them that sometimes our biggest flaws—the mistakes we make—are related to our greatest strengths. These are things we do well but are channeled in the wrong direction. If we identify what is going wrong, we can make things right using our Neurocycle superpower.

So, based on the example above, you can say something like, "I see you feel irritated with your brother a lot when he does things his way and not your way. I think this is because you really love things to be very organized and like planning the game. This is really a very smart thing you are able to do. But can you see how getting irritated with your brother makes the game less fun? How about you explain to your brother kindly so he listens to how you can make the game more fun? Maybe you can tell him how you plan to do this. Should we try to do this together? I can help you if you want."

Here are some other examples of reconceptualized statements that you can use:

You are oversensitive. = "You are aware of and honor your emotions because they are valid. There is nothing wrong with feeling deeply."

You are aggressive. = "You are passionate but do not always express this correctly. Thankfully, you are learning how to do this and are getting better every day!"

You always do that. = "You have done this in the past, but now you are learning what to do and what not to do. Your past does not define your future!"

You are useless. = "You are not someone else's definition of useful. You define what is useful for you."

No one will be able to love you with all your feelings. = "The right people will love you for who you are and for what you can offer the world. You are special!"

157

You can't get anything right. = "You know that you make mistakes, just like everyone does, and you see these mistakes as learning opportunities."

5. Active Reach

With your child, work out a simple phrase or action they can say or do that will help them practice what they learned in their Recheck. Once your child has figured this out, create a reminder to prompt them to say or do it at least seven times a day, which will help them practice the new thought—making that thought tree healthy and strong.

Remember, Active Reaches are progressive, daily growth reminders to help your child drive their changing brain in the right direction and become more self-confident.

For Ages 3–5

With your child age 3–5, try to start with something simple and go from there. An identity Active Reach for a child in this age group on day 1 of the Neurocycle could be as simple as, "I don't need to be angry anymore because I am a very special person." By day 2, this could progress into, "My toys say I am so kind and learn things so fast." By day 3, this could be, "I can help my mom at home with tidying my toys—there's lots I can do," and so on.

For Ages 6–10

With your child age 6–10, again start with something simple and doable. Try not to overwhelm your child. Remember, there is time! Identity development isn't something that can be rushed.

An identity Active Reach for this age group on day 1 of the Neurocycle could be as simple as, "I am aware that looking at other people's lives makes me feel bad about myself." By day 2, this could progress into, "I actually feel very sad when I compare my life to other people's lives, so I am just going to focus on myself and what I like for a week and see how I feel," and so on.

Additional Tips for Helping Your Child through an Identity Crisis

Below are some additional tips you may find helpful as you work through the Neurocycle with your child to help them discover and shape their identity. These also make great Active Reach prompts.

- Avoid pointing out your child's mistakes to make them feel bad and guilt them into better behavior. This is nonproductive and will make them feel ashamed. Instead, focus on the lessons they have learned from their past mistakes in a nonjudgmental way. A great way to do this is to show how you have learned from your own past mistakes.

- Remember that it's easy and common for anyone, including children, to slip in and out of how they understand themselves. It's really hard not to be affected by people's opinions and the world we live in. We won't always have a grasp on who we are, and that is okay. The key is to help your child have a mental plan in place for when they do experience moments of self-crisis so that these feelings don't take over and consume their sense of self.

- Remind yourself that you are helping them find *their* identity, not who you'd like or want them to be or who *you* think they are.

18

Social Interactions

No matter how much we try to prepare our children for the ups and downs of life, there are so many things that can hurt, especially as they interact with other people who have their own mental struggles, which is why giving our children a mental tool kit to tackle these issues from a young age is so valuable.

Social interactions are incredibly varied and complex. They can be challenging even for an adult. Now imagine you are a child and are still learning about the world and trying to understand what is going on around you. Social interactions can be tough! Thankfully, you can use the Neurocycle steps to calm your child down when they are struggling in a particular social situation or to deal with the more long-term effects of a negative social situation such as being bullied.

Remember, the Neurocycle can be used for both immediate and chronic issues. For day-to-day struggles, you can use the 5 Steps to help your child calm down and organize their thinking in the moment. For situations that have been going on for longer periods of time, such as bullying or teasing, struggles will show up in a pattern of warning signals and may require that you do the Neurocycle over several 63-day periods.

It's incredibly helpful to have a system in place to help your child manage their social interactions, because this is one of the main areas that can affect a child's mental health. No matter how much we try to prepare our children for the ups and downs of life, there are so many things that can hurt, especially as they interact with other people who have their own mental struggles, which is why giving our children a mental tool kit to tackle these issues from a young age is so valuable.

Fighting with friends, experiencing first crushes and first disappointments, failing to meet their own and other people's expectations, and other kinds of social stressors cannot be avoided. However, we can help our children learn to manage these experiences, which is what I am teaching you to do in this book! One of the best things we can do is try to listen to and acknowledge our children's sadness, anger, or frustration as they navigate their relationships with other people and walk them through embracing (Gather Awareness), processing (Reflect and Write/Play/Draw), and reconceptualizing (Recheck and Active Reach) the specific feelings that come up to find the root of the problem and make things better and more manageable so it doesn't affect their mental peace.

Bullying

As mentioned above, there are social situations that require much more advocacy and intervention, such as bullying, which is harmful on a physical, mental, and emotional level. This is unfortunately something that many children experience or participate in. It can be damaging to their well-being in the short and long term, and in all cases, it should never be ignored or suppressed.

This includes bullying experienced online. Since the advent of social media, cyberbullying has become a major issue for children as well. Parents of children who are bullied online are often not aware of everything that is going on, and even if they are, it can be hard to intervene.

According to recent statistics, "globally, one in three children have been bullied in the past 30 days."[1] Young children exposed to bullying can suffer educational, social, and health consequences, which often last well into adulthood.[2] Bullying is a form of trauma that closely connects to how a child identifies with themselves within the world and with others, how they form or make relationships, and how they learn to trust or mistrust people.[3]

Bullying prevention is a community effort and will require parents, educators, and other members of the community to work together holistically. It really does take a village—parents, teachers, therapists, psychologists, physicians, school administrators, school counselors, and others—to make an impactful change. This change needs to involve whole-home and "whole-school approaches incorporating multiple disciplines," which include strategies that "increase opportunities for positive peer interaction through carefully structured, group-based learning activities in schools" and at home.[4]

Indeed, bullying is not just a "school thing." There is a strong link between children who are bullied in school and those who are also bullied at home by their siblings.[5] Part of what a parent can do at home is to begin using the Neurocycle with the whole family, not just the child being bullied, to help mitigate and prevent negative social habits from taking root, which have the potential to spill out in how a child acts at school.

In the South African schools I worked in for over twenty years, I indirectly addressed bullying through using the Neurocycle method to help children manage their mental health and how it impacted their social interactions. This was something the children could do at school and at home with their parents or guardians. I would do this alongside teaching them the version of the Neurocycle that helps them learn how to learn (which I address in detail in my book *Think, Learn, Succeed*).

This proved to be a really helpful way of managing both the roots and the effects of bullying. It shifted the focus from a punishment-centered approach to one that balanced emotional and cognitive development through mind-management, identity, and brain-building. The students were empowered to embrace, process, and reconceptualize how they felt within themselves, which helped address the emotional neglect, unmet needs, and identity issues that had resulted in the bullying. This, in turn, developed the children's sense of empathy and recognition of their impact on others—they began to see how they were a part of a larger community. As these students learned how to learn and build their mind and brain, their creativity, confidence, and intellectual curiosity developed, which also helped them manage their feelings and internal motivations and reduce the need to bully others.

Although this may just sound like a nice story, it is something you can start doing with your child as well. The more you help them use the Neurocycle to manage their feelings and mental health, the more you will help them turn negative social demands into deep, meaningful relationships.

Empathy

One of the key ways to combat bullying is through the development of empathy in children. Empathy helps a child understand that other people have their own points of view, feelings, and emotions that need to be respected.[6] It teaches them to avoid imposing their own opinions on others and helps them understand that it is not just about them—it's about them *in the world*.

The more a child practices empathy, the more they learn to regulate their own behavior and adjust it depending on the person they are talking to and the situation they are in. In fact, studies show that by age three, children can begin to show genuine compassion and empathy and are able to understand that their feelings and experiences are different from those of others. It is never too soon to start teaching your child how to be more empathetic!

Additionally, as mentioned earlier, empathy also helps a child develop their own identity. Identity, autonomy, empathy, and resilience are all intertwined, because the more we see and understand how unique other people are, the more we learn how to recognize and value our own uniqueness. Furthermore, research confirms that children who are more skilled at being empathetic are also more skilled at communicating and therefore experience less conflicts and bullying.[7]

Empathy in children includes the following characteristics, which you may find helpful as you work on the Recheck step with your child:

- Understanding that they are a distinct person from those around them and that other people have different feelings and perspectives.
- Recognizing the feelings in themselves and others and naming them.
- Regulating their own emotional responses.
- Being able to put themselves in someone else's shoes and imagine how someone else might feel about a situation or person.
- Imagining what kind of action or response might help a person feel better in a particular situation.[8]

Empathy evolves from the time we are babies through childhood and adolescence and is fashioned by our nature, nurture, and I-factor (see chapter 16). Even though it is part of being human, it is still something we should encourage our children to practice and develop through self-regulation.

It's easy to miss the signs of a young child's sense of empathy unless we know what to look for. Young children will, for example, play in a more complex and empathic way with children they know compared to children they don't know.[9] We also see empathy reflected in the inquiries that toddlers make about what other children are going through.[10] For example, a young child may, using limited vocabulary or even a sign, ask why another child is crying.

As parents and caregivers, we can help facilitate this sense of empathy in our children through self-regulation, which is what you are doing when you work through the Neurocycle with your child. As you work through the Gathering Awareness step, you validate your child's experience as you tune in to them, which, in turn, starts teaching them the value of their feelings and the feelings of others. When you do the Reflect and Write/Play/Draw steps with your child, you are also showing them that their feelings and reactions are real and valid—their unique experiences are important. When you do the Recheck and Active Reach steps with your child, you are teaching them how their experiences and reactions are unique and that they can choose how they want to respond and who they want to be—just like other children and adults choose how they respond and what they want to be.

> **As parents and caregivers, we can help facilitate this sense of empathy in our children through self-regulation.**

Empathy has a lot to do with apologizing as well. Rather than forcing your child to say sorry, especially when they are younger and may not be able to grasp the full meaning behind an apology, you can teach them to feel empathy for the other person. For example, if your child got mad at their sibling while they were playing and hit them, and your other child is crying, you can say something like, "Look, your sister/brother is really sad and is crying (Gather Awareness). They are sore because you hit them (Reflect). Can we try to see if you can make them feel better (Recheck)? What can you do to make things better? Maybe a hug and kiss? What will you do next time you are upset (Active Reach)?"

I suggest using empathy phrases as you do the Neurocycle with your child instead of just telling them what they did that was wrong. Some good examples of this are:

"I can see that you are mad."

"I can hear that you are angry at me."

"I can see that you're feeling sad."

"It totally makes sense that you feel annoyed."

"I can see that you are feeling a lot of different feelings right now; do you want some help working through them?"

These are good examples of phrases you can say to your child to show them what it looks like to see and validate what other people are going through while you work on resolving the issue at hand.

Attachment

Social interactions are, at their core, about forming attachments and developing deep, meaningful relationships.[11] The dependent nature of children means that their family and caregivers will have a lot of influence on the way they develop and perceive their social experiences. When a child is born, they form a bond almost immediately with their caregiver. Out of this attachment, a child discovers the world—children generally see their parents as templates for living. Research shows that children hold ideal perceptions of parent figures to which they compare their own parenting and parent attachments; the interaction between these childhood expectations and the social actualization of their relationships with their parents contributes to shaping their concepts of self, self-esteem, generational beliefs, relationship dynamics, and personality overall.[12]

However, one of the most important relationships we have and attachments we form is with ourselves. This is shaped by the attachments we form in childhood. Generally, a child will experience attachment on a continuum. Some attachments will be good, fulfilling natural and deep-seated needs for deep, meaningful connections, which help a child learn how to fulfill their needs and show them how they can feel comfortable, secure, and safe; these attachments positively impact the physiological, neurological, and psychosocial development of children.[13]

Some attachments may be more neutral, but within them, there may not be enough display of affection and encouragement for children to express themselves; so, even though the child may know they are loved, they may not feel loved. Unfortunately, some attachments will be toxic and harmful, contributing to behavioral issues (e.g., ADHD), distrustful natures, generational parenting issues, and other physical and mental health problems.[14] On the extreme end, toxic attachments from childhood trauma can play out into adolescence and adulthood in a toxic way because of the plastic paradox of neuroplasticity: both the good and the bad are wired into the neural networks of the brain. However, as I have pointed out many times in this book, these negative attachments do not have to be our destiny. What was wired in can be changed (reconceptualized), including our attachments.

One of the most important relationships we have and attachments we form is with ourselves. This is shaped by the attachments we form in childhood.

It's unfair and abhorrent to have had a terrible start in life, like we saw with Tim's story. He was starved of basic loving support from his birth mother right from infancy. Instead of comforting him, she abused him. Instead of shielding him from physical pain, she hurt him *and* stood by while others hurt him. As Tim started learning how to talk, she coached him to respond with lies to cover her mistreatment when he was asked questions about his nightmares, incontinence, bruises, and ailments. When he needed medical attention, his mother ignored his pain and struggles.

However, when I sat with Tim, we had the most wonderful time. He was kind, intelligent, and well-adjusted. I was taken aback by how he seemed just like any other happy eight-year-old boy despite what he had gone through. In between talking, he played with my dogs, swam with his sister in the sea, and kept popping up with great analogies and deep questions about the mind and brain.

Tim's story shows that even if a child has a horrible start in life, this doesn't mean they are doomed for the rest of their life. His early nurturing was atrocious, and his attachments were completely distorted. However, as his phenomenal dad and stepmom demonstrate in their stories (see chapter 14), when you immerse a child in love and help them manage their mind, healing can take place and change can happen.

There is no hard-and-fast rule for what attachment should look like, which is why it is more important to cultivate a sense of safety, freedom, and autonomy within the cultural context in which your child is raised. A healthy sense of attachment, which will look different in each child and cultural environment, establishes and maintains a safe base from which a child can go out and explore the world (this is the principle of safety net parenting I spoke about in chapter 16).[15] Tim's parents created this base for him, which gave Tim the ability to start healing and exploring. By creating loving attachment, his stepmom and dad helped him find and explore what was inside of him.

Children have many cognitive skills, including cognitive flexibility, the ability to mentally multitask, and the ability to adjust their thinking upon changes in expectations or circumstances. These skills are strongest during childhood and adolescent development and decrease with age. Children can react to changes in their environment and adapt to them, and then adapt back again. However, exposure to stress and trauma in childhood impairs children's cognitive flexibility levels.[16] Thus, the sooner we teach them mind-management and self-regulation, the sooner we can also teach them how to harness this flexibility in their social interactions and form healthy attachments that help them grow and develop.

19

Social Interactions and the Neurocycle

> Using the Neurocycle with your child doesn't have to be complicated; it doesn't have to go a certain way or occur in a certain place to be effective.

As you read the story below, you'll see I wind the 5 Steps of the Neurocycle throughout to show you how this process can be used to calm yourself down as a parent when things get tough, and as a mini Neurocycle to help your child process and manage difficult social situations in the moment.

Imagine a family of five—a mom, a dad, their seven-year-old twin girls, and their ten-year-old boy—arrives at a family get-together. Just as they are about to get out of the car, one of the girls, Chantal, starts crying. Chantal's brother, frustrated because he wants to go inside to play with his cousin's new puppy, yells at her to stop crying, telling her that her face is red and splotchy. This makes things even worse, and she goes from sobbing to screaming that she doesn't want to go inside. She says that she hates the family and that she won't go in because they all tease her. They always tell her she is too skinny, is small, and wears stupid glasses. Her twin sister, Jane, starts crying as well.

The parents initially try to persuade Chantal that it will be fun, that everyone loves her, and that she looks smarter with her glasses on. They tell her that she is still growing and that she should just ignore what her cousins say. They tell her that she knows her granny loves her and will protect her and that Granny will be very sad if she doesn't come inside. However, Chantal just keeps wailing.

This angers her parents, who respond in raised tones, "You're embarrassing us. The family knows we're parked here! You're making a fuss about nothing. If we have to go home now, I'm taking your phone away from you for the whole weekend!" Jane also starts shouting. "What's the problem? I want to play with the new puppy too!" Then her brother shouts, "Why can't you be more like Jane?" As you can imagine, all this shouting only makes things a lot worse.

Then something happens. Mom notices how the situation is escalating and decides to Neurocycle. For her first Neurocycle, she works on herself. She Gathers Awareness of her and her family's frustration and how tense her body is feeling, and she observes that she is speaking in a snappy and irritated way and developing an attitude of *This day is messed up.* She then Reflects on how Chantal is acting very differently from how she usually acts, and she remembers that Chantal had complained about being teased the last time the family got together. She visualizes how upset Chantal was (remember, you can replace Writing with visualizing when dealing with something in the moment). She then Rechecks for a moment by trying to see this situation from Chantal's perspective, which helps her understand how going inside is a frightening situation for Chantal. Once she does this, it becomes easy to move into the Active Reach; she climbs into the back seat, puts her arms lovingly around her daughter, and apologizes for getting irritated with her. She explains why she did—that she is so excited to see her mom, dad, and sisters, they had been driving for a long time, and she really wants to get inside. Mom also tells Chantal that she loves her so much, that Chantal gives her so much joy just by being alive, and that this will never change no matter what Chantal says or does. All of this takes only a couple minutes and helps calm them both down.

Then Mom starts another Neurocycle, this time with Chantal, focusing on how Chantal can get through this situation. She helps her Gather Awareness of how she is feeling by saying, "I know you don't want to go inside (behavioral warning signal). Can you tell me how you are feeling right now (emotional warning signal)? Where are you feeling this in your body (bodily sensation warning signal)?" Chantal responds that she is scared and her tummy hurts. She tells her mom that her head hurts too, and she wants to cry. Mom responds by saying, "I think you are really scared to go through this teasing again, which makes you feel bad about yourself (perspective warning signal). Is that right?"

Then Mom starts Reflecting with Chantal, explaining that she understands it can be hard to be around people who make you feel bad about yourself and that what her cousins said about her was hurtful, validating Chantal's experience. She explains that this had happened to her before at work when people said something unkind, and for a while it was very hard to go back to work. Then the rest of the family suddenly begins to share their own similar experiences. Chantal, at this point, has entirely stopped crying and listens to what everyone is saying.

This prompts everyone to Reflect together on why this situation hurt Chantal and recall in their minds (Write) the scene Chantal described when she was teased. One cousin had defended her from the others, but she doesn't know if that cousin is going to be there today, so she is worried.

They then Recheck as a family how they can solve this problem. They decide Chantal will confront the cousins if they start being mean again, and her siblings will support her. She will tell them that she doesn't have great vision but gets to wear cool glasses like famous people and that even though she is skinny, she is still very strong, and that they should stop teasing her because it's unkind and makes her feel bad. They also let Chantal know that she can just tell them to stop, then walk away, because not everyone will be a good friend, and sometimes you must walk away from bad relationships if the other person doesn't want to change. They agree as a family that, if this doesn't work, her siblings will call in the adults to discuss the teasing and work it out as a group.

Then they all hug and apologize to Chantal for saying unkind things. Chantal agrees to go inside (her Active Reach), holding tightly to her twin sister's hand, confident in knowing that she has a plan to help her get through the family visit.

As they are walking up the pathway to the front door, her dad whispers, "I'm so proud of you for having the courage to face your cousins," and Chantal breaks into a big smile. Then she smiles even wider when she sees her favorite cousin and her granny waiting for her.

∎ ∎ ∎

Using the Neurocycle with your child doesn't have to be complicated; it doesn't have to go a certain way or occur in a certain place to be effective. These steps can be done very quickly in the moment when needed—they are designed to guide your thinking as you engage in a difficult situation and can be used anywhere and anytime.

Additional Tips for Helping Your Child through Social Interaction Challenges

Below are some additional tips you may find helpful as you work through the Neurocycle with your child to help them through social interaction challenges. These also make great Active Reach prompts.

- Try to really listen to your child's sadness, anger, or frustration if they are fighting with a friend. Listen to their experience and ask them if they want to fix the situation or if they think it's better to move on. Give them the choice—this will help them feel empowered and encourage them to develop their own sense of empathy rather than just relying on you to make social decisions for them. Teach them that some relationships are worth fighting for, and others are okay to end. Work with them on how moving on would look. Encourage your child to do a decompression activity once they have expressed their feelings, have all their emotions out, and have worked through the 5 Steps.

- Try to ask your child if they want advice before just giving it. Sometimes your child just wants a safe place to vent and unpack their emotions.

- Teach your child how to apologize when their words or mistakes have hurt others. This is best done by being an example for them—say sorry and explain why—and the more you do that, the better your child will become at self-regulating and knowing when to apologize.

- Remember that your child has the right to question and challenge ideas, discipline, and so on; hear them out when they do, and then guide them through the Neurocycle. You can even show them how to use the Neurocycle to challenge something in an organized and nonaggressive way.

- Be kind to yourself—raising children isn't easy! If you can look back and realize *I didn't do that so well. I didn't have to get angry right at that moment. I could've been more responsive, or I could've said or done that differently*, talk about this with your child. This shows your child what insight and introspection look like, which gives you a chance to repair and grow the relationship. We need to acknowledge the impact of what we have done but also balance this with our intentions. We want the best for our children, but we also need to remember that we are humans going through our own "stuff," which can cloud our judgment.

20

■■■■■■■■

Labels

Your child is not lost or "broken." If they have received a bunch of labels, instead of seeing these labels as your child's brain diseases, see them as descriptions of the warning signals your child is exhibiting.

Imagine your child is the new kid in class. They are being bullied, and you have noticed changes in their behavior. They are not able to concentrate as well in class or at home, they are getting increasingly distracted, they have greater anxiety, they are unable to sit still, especially in calm or quiet surroundings, they are constantly fidgeting, they talk excessively and are unable to wait their turn, they often act without thinking, and they have started interrupting conversations.

Are these symptoms of a brain disease or warning signals that something is going wrong in your child's life that is impacting their mental and physical well-being? What do you do as a parent? Who do you listen to?

A Labeling Story

One of my patients, whom I will call John, went through this exact experience. In the early 2000s, ten-year-old John walked into my practice with his mom. He had been getting a series of bad grades and was beginning to feel that he was hopeless at school. He constantly felt the urge to move, so he would wiggle and shift in his seat and frequently ask to go to the restroom, not because he needed to go but because he needed to move.

As you can imagine, he got into a lot of trouble with his teachers. He was referred to the school psychologist, who diagnosed him with ADHD (attention deficit hyperactivity disorder) and referred him to a psychiatrist for medication after merely reading the report from a teacher—she didn't even take the time to talk to John. All the psychiatrist did was ask a few questions from a checklist in a brief fifteen-minute period before prescribing medication and telling them to come back in a few weeks.

John's mom took him back to the psychiatrist several days later because he was losing a great deal of weight from the ADHD medication, which was suppressing his appetite. He had also started experiencing depressive symptoms. They were told by the psychiatrist that his "brain disease" was getting worse and that he needed an antidepressant as well. This combination made him feel suicidal and agitated on top of feeling depressed, and when the psychiatrist wanted to add an antipsychotic to his medication regimen, the mom said no—and this is when they came to my clinical practice.

I sat down with John and asked him to tell me his story. John said that when he moved, it helped him focus, and he found it really hard to concentrate and process what the teachers were saying when he was told to sit still and stop fidgeting. Additionally, he was growing very quickly and was much taller than his classmates and very skinny. He was also teased a lot by his peers because he went to the restroom so frequently. This made him feel really sad, and he was also embarrassed about his grades. Between the teasing, the teacher picking on him constantly, the embarrassment, and now being labeled and told he had a broken brain—while trying to understand his mood swings and deal with his loss of appetite and energy from the medication—he felt helpless and worthless, like he was a failure at everything.

When John walked into my office, he was hunched over, his hair was covering his eyes, and he wouldn't look me in the eye—he was trying to hide as much as he could. Once I got him telling his story, however, the floodgates opened. His sense of shame was consuming him. He felt as if he was being scrutinized at every turn by his teachers, his peers, and his stay-at-home mom, who was so worried about him and tried to protect him, while his father expected nothing less than perfection and always compared him to his sibling, who just seemed to get everything right.

The first thing I did after hearing John's story was to complete an identity Neurocycle with him to help him understand his value and self-worth, which we worked on for the first few sessions. We also swapped out his desk chair in class for a Pilates ball, which gave him the rocking motion his brain needed. As a result, his focus and concentration improved, which had a great impact on his ability to think. Over several weeks, notwithstanding his struggles, John also learned how to use the Neurocycle system to manage his thoughts and feelings, which helped him regulate his emotions and movements.

We completed many family Neurocycles to help with the toxic dynamics. Mom learned to shift to safety net parenting instead of helicopter parenting, which she had slipped into purely as a way to protect her child. Dad realized that comparing siblings had not achieved his intention of motivating his son and had actually made John feel worse about himself. Instead, he learned how to validate John as a person, help him rebuild his identity, and assist him with his schoolwork.

Moreover, as John also learned how to use the Neurocycle to learn (see my book *Think, Learn, Succeed* for more on this), he was able to improve his grades to the point that he started helping other children in his class learn. This exchange of roles rapidly shifted the respect dynamics in the classroom. I then referred them to a doctor who helped John taper off his medication and to an endocrinologist to check his hormones, which helped him feel better and start eating again. We also started family and individual therapy sessions to address his learning and emotional challenges.

How This Story Can Help You

John and I worked together for close to a year, so we completed approximately five 63-day Neurocycles. Throughout this process, he learned how to trust himself again and discover his unique potential and self-regulation superpowers. He didn't get stuck in a label. He blossomed into a happy, well-adjusted young man. I wish John's story could be every child's story, but too often that isn't the case. Currently, the average age of initial ADHD diagnosis is seven years old,[1] and from 2000 to 2015 the rate of stimulant prescription increased 800 percent.[2] It's estimated that only about 1 to 2 percent of children qualify[3] as having symptoms of ADHD, but up to 15 percent are being diagnosed, with this figure climbing every year;[4] for instance, there has been a fiftyfold increase in pre-scribing ADHD drugs in just twenty years. Across the board, more and more children are being diagnosed, labeled, and medicated.

Is diagnosing, labeling, and medicating actually helping the children? A recent study[5] observed that ADHD meds don't lead to higher grades or more learning, which is something I witnessed with John and with many of the children and adults I have worked with over the years. Indeed, a lot of research shows that taking ADHD medications like Ritalin is associated with an increased risk of depression[6] and suicide in children who also take antidepressants.[7]

It's important to understand that the symptoms of ADHD or ADD (attention deficit disorder) are nonspecific and common in the general population.[8] There is no clearly defined boundary sepa-rating a high-spirited child with average levels of hyperactivity, impulsivity, and distractibility from a child who is really battling to concentrate and learn. These labels are inherently imprecise and subjective and don't point to an underlying specific biological cause as is implicated—the judgment is very much in the eye of the beholder. In fact, there are wide individual differences in the normal distribution of these features across any given population, which also differ wildly across families, schools, and cultural levels of tolerance.

Is there evidence that the current system of diagnoses and labels based on a purely biomedical approach is helping children? If so, we should certainly keep using this approach. However, if the evidence suggests we are doing more harm than good, and if the labeling and diagnosing of children leaves many children stigmatized and disempowered,[9] then situating a child's issues within the complicated narrative of a child's life and contextualizing their behaviors is by far the better option.

Symptoms as Signals

Having researched this question for over three decades, including in my clinical practice from the late '80s to the mid-2000s, I believe the evidence supports the second option. In my master's thesis and research,[10] I observed significant improvement across different age groups in academic, cognitive, social, and emotional functioning by up to 75 percent when teaching children to focus on managing their mind within the context of their life. I also observed this in over twenty years of working in government-run schools in South Africa.

In one of my studies applying the Neurocycle for learning within a charter school system in Dallas, Texas, my team and I found that students' academic scores improved significantly in reading (25 percent) and math (22 percent) for fifth grade and in math (11 percent) and reading (9 percent) for eighth grade.[11] These results confirmed that teaching children how to harness the power of their innate abilities to think and learn by mastering their bio-psycho-social reality can help them overcome many school struggles and avoid labels of school failure.

Over the years, I have noticed a significant surge in labeling and medicalizing childhood distress and immaturity. In my first years of practicing, I worked closely with a team of professionals, parents, and caregivers to determine the story of each child and to understand the source and the context of their issues. This was an ongoing, organic process that took place over weeks and even months. Neurological and biological considerations were *part of* the investigation, not the overarching assumption directing the process. We understood that the symptoms we were observing were signals that became established patterns over time and that had become severe enough to interfere with a child's functioning on multiple levels. These are things that cannot be investigated or managed in a fifteen- or thirty-minute session with a checklist.

> **Psychiatric diagnoses can be useful if they are seen as descriptions of symptoms and warning signals.**

Psychiatric diagnoses can be useful if they are seen as descriptions of symptoms and warning signals. However, they are not purely explanatory, and they do not define a clear biological state such as cancer or diabetes. To say that a child is having a "manic episode" is to simply provide a name for or categorize certain observable behaviors, such as throwing a tantrum or running around uncontrollably. Likewise, to say that a child has ADHD is to simply provide a name for or categorize certain observable behaviors, such as battling to pay attention or being easily distractible and hyperactive.

We do our children a disservice when we don't take the time to elaborate on the context of each of these symptoms and ask who, what, how, when, where, and why. *How often does this happen? What are their triggers? Are there times they do pay attention?* We should look at everything holistically before a diagnosis is made.

This should include waiting and observing, getting advice, parent and caregiver training, environmental changes, stress reduction, how-to-learn skills, and therapy.

Of course, this mental health approach takes time and resources to complete well. Unfortunately, the "consideration of the complex and long-term implications of childhood relationships does not sit comfortably in a cash-strapped, time-strapped, evidence-based, label-based, protocol-based system."[12] However, our children's life stories are way too complex for neat boxes.

As researcher and mental health advocate Dr. Peter Gøtzsche points out, "If a lion attacks us, we get terribly frightened and produce stress hormones, but this doesn't prove that it was the stress hormones that made us scared. It was the lion. No genetic predisposition or 'chemical imbalance' is needed for this [stress response]."[13] Thus, if we just look at the stress response and its effects on a child's mind and body, we will miss the "lion," which could end up causing them a lot of harm in the short and long term.

Many of the labels in the *Diagnostic and Statistical Manual of Mental Disorders* (DSM) were created by a council of experts who made largely subjective decisions regarding labels and their associated symptoms based on their experiences, which is one reason why this manual changes frequently. The late Paula Caplan, a clinical researcher, psychologist, and former consultant to the DSM, noted pointedly:

> An undeserved aura of scientific precision surrounds the [DSM] manual: It has "statistical" in its title and includes a precise-seeming three-to-five-digit code for every diagnostic category and subcategory, as well as lists of symptoms a patient must have to receive a diagnosis. But what it does is simply connect certain dots, or symptoms—such as sadness, fear or insomnia—to construct diagnostic categories that lack scientific grounding. Many therapists see patients through the DSM prism, trying to shoehorn a human being into a category.[14]

We need to remember that although categories are helpful when trying to understand and manage the human experience, no singular category can sum up an individual's human experience. As the saying goes, it's a lot more complicated than that.

Beyond Biomedical

Yes, a diagnosis and label can seem to be useful, but there is a dark side. Labels tend to influence how parents and caregivers expect their child to act. They can shape societal norms that box children in, often laying blame at the individual child's feet (or in this case, brain), increasing stigma and self-blame because they restrict the problem to a damaged brain or "broken" biology.[15] A label can send children the message that there is something fundamentally wrong with them, which is incredibly disempowering and can further exacerbate mental health issues because the diagnosis and label have changed their sense of self.[16]

There are many holes in the current biomedical mental health system and the way it treats our children. Studies in several countries have shown that the youngest child in a class is twice as likely as the oldest to get an ADHD diagnosis.[17] Many children also get the wrong diagnosis because diagnoses are unreliable, or they're given medication they don't need.[18] We are all subjected to omnipresent direct-to-consumer advertising of medications and the commercialization of psychiatric disorders. Clearly, something has to change.

Fortunately, a growing number of scientists and clinicians are criticizing this biomedical approach.[19] Recently, a retraction in *Lancet Psychiatry* was called for based on misleading research that falsely professed to show a biological cause for ADHD.[20] Even the so-called father of ADHD, Keith Conners, whose research laid the foundation for the field of child psychopharmacology and converted what was once an indeterminate condition (called Minimal Brain Dysfunction, or MBD) into the now widely accepted and

DSM-official diagnosis of ADHD,[21] and Dr. Allen Frances, former chairman of the DSM-IV task force who helped codify ADHD into the DSM, have come out as outspoken critics of the overdiagnosis, labeling, and increased medicating of children. As Frances notes, "It is disheartening to see diagnoses that are useful for the few become harmful when misapplied for the many."[22] Much of what we call science in the field of mental health isn't really that scientific at all. According to child and adolescent psychiatrist Sami Timimi, "Our professional constructs (such as the diagnoses used by psychiatrists, psychologists and others), do not reflect any advance in 'scientific' discovery, but [are] just another set . . . of cultural beliefs and practices" that can "have many negative, unintended consequences."[23]

Indeed, "diagnoses like ADHD reflect . . . the tendency to problematize 'childish' behaviors and then 'medicalize' them, sparing all concerned from the more difficult task of accepting, understanding and supporting the imperfect and often contradictory ways children develop and find emotional security."[24]

It is up to us as parents and caregivers to go beyond this limited mental health framework and to advocate for our children.

Timimi's work, alongside that of many other mental health professionals and advocates like him, highlights the lack of evidence supporting the idea that biomedical psychiatric diagnoses are always valid and always reliable.[25] Many of the current diagnostic categories used in child psychiatry tell you very little about what is going on with your child, whether you are talking about the cause, treatment, or outcome. Professor Timimi explains in depth, in his numerous books and research papers on this subject, how, in fact, the manufacturing of ADHD has come about. There is no characteristic genetic abnormality, brain imaging studies have not uncovered any specific characteristic abnormality, nor is there a characteristic chemical imbalance associated with ADHD.[26]

It is up to us as parents and caregivers to go beyond this limited mental health framework and to advocate for our children, which is why I wrote this book. I wanted to give you the ability to help your child manage their many complicated life experiences in a way that doesn't place an unnecessary burden of blame on their shoulders or make them feel damaged or less worthy.

21

Labels and the Neurocycle

> Your child is not lost or "broken." If they have received a bunch of labels, instead of seeing these labels as your child's brain diseases, see them as descriptions of the warning signals your child is exhibiting.

Now we'll go through how to use the Neurocycle for labeling. You can help your child learn how to manage their mind and practice self-regulation if they have been unfairly locked in or stigmatized by a label.

Again, I recommend recording your observations and insights in a journal as you work through the Neurocycle. This can be incredibly helpful if you are working through these issues with a child therapist or mental health professional.

1. Gather Awareness

Say your child has been labeled with ADHD, bipolar depression, pediatric bipolar or general anxiety disorder, autism, or even a few of these diagnoses. You may ask the mental health professional why they have these labels, and the answer you receive will be a list of symptoms (which often are similar to the ones you told the mental health professional in the first place). This is what happened to John's parents. He was given more than eight diagnoses in a fifteen-minute visit with the psychiatrist, mostly based on his mom filling out a questionnaire, and with very little interaction with John himself.

Of course, not every psychiatrist will do this. I know of a few great professionals who focus on a child's story rather than just medicalizing them using a symptom list. It is, however, of great concern that this happens more often than it should, especially in light of the questionable validity and reliability of diagnosis and labeling within the biomedical mental health model discussed in the previous chapter.

If John's story sounds familiar, I want to tell you there is hope. Your child is not lost or "broken." If they have received a bunch of labels, instead of seeing these labels as your child's brain diseases, see them as descriptions of the warning signals your child is exhibiting, as discussed in part 1. These signals are pointing to a thought or a series of linked thoughts that have an origin story or stories—the roots of your child's thought trees.

First do your own Neurocycle of what you observe in your child, including what their teachers or mental health professionals have said to you. Gather Awareness of the four warning signals so that you will have the language needed to help your child describe what they are experiencing.

Remember, these are not symptoms pointing to a label! They are words describing your child's experience. Here are some examples:

- *Emotional warning signals*: frustrated, angry, irritable, bored, excited, mood swings, sad, depressed, anxious
- *Behavioral warning signals*: aggressive, fidgety, impulsive, withdrawn, erratic self-control, loses focus and attention, forgetful

- *Bodily sensation warning signals*: upset tummy, gastrointestinal issues, headaches, sore arms or legs
- *Perspective warning signals*: doesn't want to go to school because they hate it, have stopped enjoying life because they feel lost

Before you start doing the Neurocycle with your child and asking them about their warning signals, you can explain that you also did the Neurocycle so you could better understand and help them and have noticed that they _____ (list some of the signals). Ask them if this is indeed what they are feeling. Based on their age, use demonstration, images, pictures, and words to do this.

Emphasize and explain to your child that they are not bad and that you are not upset with them. Let them know that they have done nothing wrong and that you love them so much no matter what they do or say and no matter what someone else says about them. Explain that there is a reason and a solution for everything that's happening in their life right now, and that you will find this out together to make things better. Explain why you may have been upset, and make sure they know it's not because of something they did or because they are a bad person.

For Ages 3–5

Children ages 3–5 need to know that it's okay if they are not always performing at a peak or desired level and that it's safe to get upset or angry every once in a while, without fear of being judged for it. Guiding them through the process of expressing the four warning signals will help you tune in to them and help them express themselves in a safe way.

So instead of saying, "You are a grumpy boy today," say something like, "I see you are feeling grumpy." Next, frame the warning signals as observations and not labels. This knowledge will give them the freedom to connect with who they truly are and to connect with you to explore whatever they are experiencing in the moment.

Remember, by avoiding labeling children, we are giving them their best chance to become the people they were born to be. Make sure to give your child as much space and time as they need to work on Gathering Awareness of how they feel as you work through this step of the Neurocycle with them.

For Ages 6–10

Instead of labeling your child as pediatric bipolar, as having ADHD, or whatever term they have received, try to help them describe the warning signals they are experiencing by saying something like, "Are you feeling _____ and saying _____ because of _____?"

The same principle applies to other descriptions. Instead of saying "You are shy" or "Don't be shy," for example, try to use statements such as, "It takes a little while for you to feel comfortable with new people," or "You are talkative with people you know well." Try to be as descriptive as possible without giving your child any one label—even with positive statements! Instead of labeling your child as "brave" or "helpful," for instance, try to say something like, "You are acting so brave," or "She was very brave when she did that."

When a child is negatively labeled, people's expectations of them are lowered, and the child may not be adequately challenged or receive the opportunities needed to reach their potential. The same is true for a positive label, which can burden a child with certain expectations and make them feel that if they don't meet the ideals of the label, they are not worthy. This can put them under severe pressure to constantly perform, which can be equally detrimental to their development.[1]

Labeling a child at this age can influence the way others see and treat them as well as the way they see and treat themselves. Labeling a child will have a huge impact on their self-esteem. When a person hears something about themselves often enough, they eventually start to believe it and act accordingly.[2] Always remember to tell your child, "You are not that label. The label is just a description for how you are behaving now because of _____, but it isn't how you will always be."

2. Reflect

Next, go through each of the four warning signals you identified with your child in Step 1 and ask yourself:

- Why is my child exhibiting these signals?
- What do they actually mean?
- When do they happen?
- What triggers them?
- How long do they happen?
- How do they combine together?
- Which ones seem to be interfering the most with their schoolwork?
- Which ones seem to be interfering the most with their relationships?
- Can they be linked to a specific event such as a new grade level, a new teacher, a new friend, a change in family dynamics, a traumatic experience, or bullying?

This step helps give you a general idea of the pattern and the "because" behind the way your child is behaving and what the root story could be. Next, Reflect with your child and talk about why you think they have these signals, asking them if you are correct or how they would describe themselves and why they think this is happening.

For Ages 3–5

Try not to fence your child in if they don't seem to fit what's expected of them at this stage of their life. Always consider your child's uniqueness when trying to understand their warning signals. Remember, they have so much learning and growing to do—their warning signals are not fixed. Given the right support and conditions, your child can learn and grow from their experiences.

At this age, when working on the Reflect step, you can encourage your child to playact or use toys to express what they are feeling. You can say something like, "I think your toy won't listen to the teacher because they are still learning how to go to school and not stay at home. It's not the same, is it?"

For Ages 6–10

Encourage a child age 6–10 to talk about how they feel and ask lots of questions. Discuss the warning signals as descriptions rather than attaching a label to them. For example, you can say something like, "You worked really hard on this project and feel very frustrated" rather than "You have a concentration problem."

3. Write/Play/Draw

When dealing with the impact a mental health label can have on you and your child, I really cannot recommend enough that you write down your experiences and feelings as you go through the Neurocycle on your own. All kinds of things will surface as you try to help your child. For example, you may want to write down how disconcerted you felt leaving the psychiatrist's office thinking you have a child whose brain is damaged, or you may want to write down how you question if this is your fault, and how guilty and anxious this makes you feel. This will help you manage your own feelings so that they do not negatively impact your child as you work through the Neurocycle with them. As I have mentioned many times, the well-being of your child is dependent on your well-being.

As you do this step, also remember to write down the four warning signals you Gathered Awareness of and Reflected on about your child and ask yourself why. Deconstruct each to find what you think is the context and cause. You can do this alone, with a partner, or even with a therapist. Remember, you need to take care of your own mental health as well!

Next, work on the Write/Play/Draw step with your child.

For Ages 3–5

Let your child age 3–5 draw, act, or use pictures related to what you have Gathered Awareness of and Reflected on to organize their thinking and find out more about how they feel about their label and themselves. You can help them do this by taking the pictures or words they chose from the warning signal boxes and sticking them into a journal and by helping them add more pictures or words as they think of more things connected to how they feel. You can also ask your child if they want to act this out with their toys.

Based on the example in Step 2 above, you can now playact, for example, "Let's show how Brain-ee acts at home and how Brain-ee acts at school—how can we help Brain-ee at school?"

Your child doesn't have to write, play, or draw a lot in each session, and sometimes you may do most of it, but they are watching and learning as you model this for them. Take it slow and remember to use the decompression exercises from chapter 7 if your child starts to get upset or feels stressed out.

For Ages 6–10

Encourage your child age 6–10 to write down their warning signals, helping them as needed. Next, go through each one and ask why they have this warning signal. What is it telling them about how they feel about school, life, relationships, and themselves? Your child can also draw how they feel if they prefer and use words as a support.

4. Recheck

First, Recheck the information from Steps 1–3 on your own. Ask yourself a lot of questions! Is your child perhaps having a normal childhood reaction to all the changes that have happened in your lives recently? Are they trying to process the stress you are both feeling? Is a little voice questioning your child's diagnosis and label because you *know* your child? You also know that your child is struggling at school, but maybe that's due to boredom because at home they are reading advanced books and can have long, detailed discussions about what they like. Is their school really meeting their needs?

Next, examine what you have written down and explored, noting all the things your child *can* do well in addition to where and when they function best. How can you encourage your child to do more of this?

Next, work on this step with your child.

For Ages 3–5

If your child is age 3–5 and you are using a toy like the Brain-ee doll to help them do the Neurocycle, you can say something like, "What are all the things your toy likes to do best? What is it best at? I think your toy is *so* good at ____. Am I right?"

Encourage them to do more of what they love to do and what makes them feel good about themselves. Then look at the things they are battling with to see what can be done to help them. For example, maybe they struggled to finish a puzzle at school, which makes them feel like they are bad at school. You could find time to practice puzzles with them at home to help them improve. Or perhaps your child gets distracted easily, so you could sit with them and help them practice listening to stories (such as with an audiobook) and encourage them to imagine all the scenes in their mind, which will help them develop their focusing skills.

For Ages 6–10

Recheck what you both worked on in Steps 1–3 together by looking at the patterns you identified and asking your child if this is what they also noticed and think is happening.

Work out ways together to take advantage of all the good things they do well. You can say something like, "Let's make a list together of all the things you are learning to do so well. Let's write as much as we can. Can I go first? I think you are so good at telling stories and get so excited when you tell them! I especially loved the story about _____. What do you think you are good at?"

Then look at the things they are struggling with to see what can be done to help them. You can say something like, "I know you are struggling to concentrate in this class. Maybe because it's boring? But you know so much about _____ and can read books about _____ so well. How can you take this excellent skill into the class you don't like?"

5. Active Reach

To help your child overcome a label using the Neurocycle, a good Active Reach would help them practice focusing on their story instead of a name or adjective that someone else has used to describe them.

For Ages 3–5

For your child age 3–5, choose something from the tips below or something you Rechecked with your child in Step 4 and practice this for a few days. For example, if your child has been labeled with ADHD because of a lack of concentration, you can listen to an audiobook together when you are making dinner, and they can draw what they hear while listening. Another Active Reach could be to go to the local library with your child each week and let them choose books for you to read to them every night at bedtime. You can even ask them questions about the book or ask them if they want to draw or playact what they think the book is about.

For Ages 6–10

A helpful Active Reach for a child age 6–10 could be to learn something new and build their brain, which will help them feel more resilient and confident in themselves and their abilities. For example, based on what I mentioned in Step 4 above, if they are struggling at school but love learning about sharks, you can encourage them to learn all the information they can about sharks and talk about the topic with their friends and teachers at school. As with younger ages, you could also go to the local library with your child each week and let them choose books that you read to them every night at bedtime, asking them questions regarding what they think the book is about.

Additional Tips for Helping Your Child Overcome the Impact of a Label

Below are some additional tips you may find helpful as you work through the Neurocycle with your child to help them overcome a diagnosis and label. These also make great Active Reach prompts.

- Consider getting language and auditory processing assessments and therapy if needed for your child, or if recommended, from a speech and language therapist.
- Look at other options for learning support if you feel this is needed. For example, a grandparent or nanny may be able to help by sitting with your child and helping them learn how to read or work through the Neurocycle to learn their homework.
- If possible, look at other schooling options such as changing schools or going to a school that uses different learning

philosophies, such as classical education or Montessori. You may even want to consider homeschooling if you can. If you choose to homeschool, you could reach out to a child psychologist or speech language therapist for help, because this can be quite daunting as a parent. Just remember to ask questions about their philosophy before you start, to make sure they won't push you just to label and medicate your child.

- Help your child find the good side of getting something wrong. You can say something like, "I agree you were very active at school today, which disturbed some other kids, so now you have learned what not to do. You have learned what disturbs the kids in your class. Now let's work out what you can do when you feel all this energy in your body. You can move a bit more on your Pilates ball, or you can imagine you are a giant and they are tiny like ants, and you need to be very quiet and move very little so that you don't squash them."

- Remember, the child struggling with self-regulation (see chapter 6) is generally the child who gets labeled because they are battling to manage the big warning signals in their emotions and body and behaviors. It's harder and more "in your face" when they battle to filter distractions or to control the impulse to move or speak. Too often, the constant moving, asking questions, and drawing on the board are labeled as bad behaviors. However, they aren't trying to be difficult or to aggravate the adults and other children; they are needing to develop their self-regulatory skills. This is where using the Neurocycle for mind-management and brain-building helps tremendously.

22

■■■■■■■■

Sleep Issues

Constantly worrying about your child's sleep patterns and identifying and labeling them as a poor sleeper may be worse than their not sleeping because of all the anxiety associated with the situation.

Getting your child to go to sleep and stay asleep can be a challenge! Bedtimes, nightmares, distractions, and many other factors can make sleep time a highly stressful situation. Compounding this stress is the constant messaging we receive that our children need more sleep. Numerous websites, articles, and medical professionals have focused on all the possible negative effects of what will happen if a child doesn't get enough sleep, which can make things even more scary.

Notably, though, sleep has a much more bidirectional relationship to well-being than was previously assumed. While a lack of quality sleep can contribute to mental and physical health struggles, the reverse is also true.[1] Children exposed to traumas such as abuse or bullying or daily life stressors on a constant basis may sleep less or have poorer quality sleep.[2] There are also a number of other reasons children don't or can't sleep well, including biological and neurological issues. When dealing with a sleep issue, it's important to look holistically at the context of a child's life.

Remember Tim's story (see chapter 14)? Notwithstanding many interventions and treatments, he continued sleeping no more than four nonconsecutive hours per night; complaining of hot flashes, leg pains, and nightmares; and battling with incontinence. It was impossible for him to attend traditional school.

This is a very real issue for many parents, caregivers, and children, and as such, it needs to be addressed as soon as possible from as many different vantage points as possible, of which mind-management is arguably the most important. Our mind drives everything else.

Sleep Disturbances

Sleep disturbances are intricately intertwined with a child's mental and physical well-being.[3] Sleep disturbances that can occur in children ages 1–12 include obstructive sleep apnea (1–5 percent), sleepwalking (17 percent), confused arousals (17.3 percent), sleep terrors (1–6.5 percent), and nightmares (10–50 percent).[4] Obstructive sleep apnea is when a child's breathing is blocked (either partially or completely) while asleep. Some signs that your child may be struggling with sleep apnea are snoring, coughing, pauses in breathing, loud mouth breathing, and restlessness.[5] Sleepwalking is an action a child does while remaining in a sleep state.[6] Confused arousals are when a child is still asleep but will cry out or thrash; they can even have a "fit" or mumble or say sentences while asleep. Sleep terrors can also result in moaning or crying out in sleep. Your child may appear restless yet be in a state of deep sleep—they are not easily aroused. While children may remember a nightmare, they tend to forget sleep terrors.[7]

Technology and Sleep

We are all familiar with the link between misuse of technology and reduced sleep. This is something that affects both children and adults. If the color settings in the device display settings are not modified, most modern technology emits a blue light wave that provokes alertness and performance in the viewer; this light specifically affects the sleep-wake cycle by decreasing melatonin production.[8] The modality and content of the screen interaction also impact children's sleep; for instance, playing video games increases children's sleep-onset latency (how long it takes them to fall asleep), decreases deep restorative (slow wave) sleep, and decreases time spent asleep.[9]

As mentioned earlier, our brain merges with whatever we focus on. This focus can boost mind and brain activity and improve sleep—or upset the neural networks and endocrine system, which can result in disturbed sleep patterns. Modern technology and social media are not necessarily the main or only culprits. On average, children don't get enough sleep; early wake-ups for school or day care and late bedtimes due to work and extracurricular activities have significantly compromised the average number of hours children sleep.[10] This fast-paced life complication has been growing since it was first mentioned in 1884 by the *British Medical Journal* in an article that attributed the rising number of children's sleep issues to the rapid nature of the growing modern society.[11] Thus, the notion that children are not sleeping because they are too distracted and overstimulated by social media or the internet alone fails to take into account that the fast pace of life, though encouraged by these technologies, isn't new and has been a source of conversation for many years.

> **Every generation faces changes that inevitably impact the pace of life because our environments are constantly evolving.**

However, this is the first time in human history that we have had to deal with social media, the internet, and the very "online" nature of modern technology, and we are still trying to figure it out.

Advice on what to do as a parent or caregiver constantly changes, which can make it hard to keep up.

Every generation faces changes that inevitably impact the pace of life because our environments are constantly evolving. This is why it's so important that we learn how to manage our mind from a young age. Life is constantly changing and throwing things at us, and we need to help both ourselves and our children learn how to manage these changes.

It is important to remember that sleep is dynamic. This means it will change as a child ages, and it will constantly be influenced by the context of a child's life. Sleep patterns will change as children go through different life events and major transitions and as they are exposed to stress.[12] As a parent or caregiver, we cannot always prevent these changes from affecting our children's well-being, but we can help them manage how these changes impact them.

How Many Hours of Sleep Does a Child Need?

I'm often asked if there is a magic number of hours children need to sleep. The answer is complicated, like pretty much everything about raising children! Furthermore, having rules that are too regimented about sleep can end up doing more harm than good. It can make a child who is having trouble sleeping feel like there is something inherently wrong with them, whether this is attributed to a biological problem or a behavioral issue, and can quickly box a child in with a label.

Indeed, a lack of quality sleep is often one of the first explanations given to a parent or caregiver to explain why their child is struggling emotionally, which means a lack of sleep often becomes pathologized, complicating matters rather than helping to solve them.[13] Sleep disturbances are generally on the top of the list of things a parent or caregiver *should* consider if their child is acting out behaviorally or expressing sadness, anger, frustration, withdrawal, and so on. Thus, this can quickly become a stressful conundrum: if your child is struggling to sleep, and you are told the cause of their problem is lack of sleep and the solution is to get them more sleep lest they fall apart mentally and physically, it is easy to panic and feel helpless. However, we need to be careful to avoid medicalizing and overproblematizing a lack of sleep for children.

While we all agree that sleep is necessary for our mental and physical well-being, and it may very well be one of the causes of a behavioral issue that a child is struggling with, it can be frustrating and stressful when we are told that our child just needs to "sleep more." Look back at Tim's story and the challenges he had with sleeping and the kinds of advice and extreme lengths his parents had to go to just to get him to sleep for a few hours. The situation can quickly become a literal nightmare.

We need to be careful to avoid medicalizing and over-problematizing a lack of sleep for children.

However, just four days into Neurocycling, Tim started sleeping better. When I asked Tim about this, his answer took me by surprise. He said, "Dr. Leaf, I love benchmark days. You said day 4 is a benchmark day for change. On day 4, I did have this change—with my mom's help, I started seeing my nightmares were why I couldn't sleep, and I started feeling like I could make them go away, and they couldn't control me anymore. That's when it just suddenly became easier to fall asleep."

When we focus on only a symptom as the root cause of an issue, we can often miss the bigger picture. One thing I used to tell the parents in my practice was to see a child's struggles as an iceberg: you see only the tip, but there is a lot more going on underneath the water. The great thing about the mind-management techniques I talk about in this book is that they help you and your child see the rest of the iceberg (or the roots of the thought trees) so that you both can understand the context of your child's life and why they are struggling. This is the key to lasting change.

Still, you may be wondering, *How many hours exactly should my child sleep at night? Is there a magic number?* There is a large body of research on this topic, dating as far back as the late nineteenth century. However, despite all these studies, we still don't have an exact consensus on how many hours of sleep children need each night.[14] While there is no doubt that sleep is associated with many benefits, including increased energy and focus and the regeneration of important psychological and physiological functions,[15] much of the advice given to parents and caregivers on the number of hours a child needs to sleep comes from debate.[16] In other words, there is no magic number! Your child will need a unique amount based on their individual physiological, neurological, psychological, and environmental needs.

When it comes to your child's sleep patterns, it's important to treat them as an individual with unique experiences and needs. When you feel stressed or fearful, or when your child feels stressed or fearful, remind yourself that there is no *one* correct way of sleeping or correct sleep pattern. In fact, children in different countries have variable sleep patterns depending on where they are from. For example, children from Europe sleep, on average, around 20–60 minutes more than children from America, and around 60–120 minutes more than children from Asian countries.[17]

Additionally, sleep isn't a constant state at all. New research shows that the expectation that a good night means uninterrupted sleep is incorrect. The neurotransmitters noradrenaline and norepinephrine, in concert, wake us up more than one hundred times a night but for such a fleeting moment that we don't notice.[18] Noradrenaline refreshes us and norepinephrine wakes us. This combination resets the brain so that it's ready to stabilize memory when we fall back asleep and also helps us wake up rested. In essence, the more we manage our mind, the more we can benefit from this cycle.

The idea that sleep research is constantly evolving in a direction of uniqueness of the individual is hopeful and a relief to the parent whose child struggles to sleep. I believe that removing "sleep expectations" can also help to remove any toxic stress and anxiety surrounding sleep, which in turn can lead to massive improvements in the actual quality of your child's sleep—and yours. Instead of worrying about a child getting a certain number of hours of sleep every night, it's better to focus our energy and attention on helping a child find their unique sleep pattern. This includes walking them through the negative associations they may have developed regarding sleep, why that is, and what else may be going on in their life.

Toxic Stress and Sleep

Sleep disturbances, as well as the stress surrounding falling asleep, can be very stressful for children, which can have a snowball effect and exacerbate their sleep issues. One of the physical effects of unmanaged stress in the brain and body is an overactive hypothalamic pituitary axis (HPA; see the image below), which is the stress regulator in the brain and body.[19] This can lead to increased levels of cortisol and adrenaline and decreased levels of melatonin,[20] which, in turn, can result in panic-induced adrenaline rushes that make a child suddenly sit up wide-eyed and awake in bed. If this happens consistently over a period of time, this stress response can lead to increased anxiety, depression, acting out, withdrawing, and other behaviors.[21]

If you are constantly exposed to knowledge about the negative risks associated with a lack of sleep, this can also make your child's sleep issues more urgent and stressful. Indeed, constantly worrying about your child's sleep patterns and identifying and labeling your child as a poor sleeper may be worse than their not sleeping because of all the anxiety associated with the situation. The expectation that things will go wrong and the subsequent sleep issues can be wired into the brain as a neural network, and before you know it, 63 days have passed and expecting poor sleep has become a "practiced" habit!

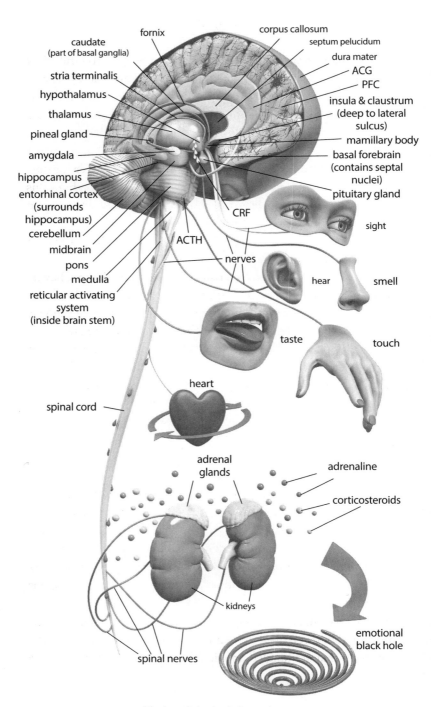

The hypothalamic pituitary axis

This is not to say that sleep issues are not real or stressful. They are! The American Academy of Pediatrics estimates that 25–50 percent of children have sleep issues,[22] a number that continues to rise each year. Despite all the time and money spent on solving "the sleep problem" with sleep aids and other cures, it is still an issue.[23]

Yet when overmedicalization changes normal aspects of the human condition, we don't necessarily make life better for ourselves or our children. As you have been learning throughout this book, a child's brain is neuroplastic and can change. Your child has the ability—using Brain-ee's superpower, the Neurocycle—to work through specific struggles and overcome them through mind-management. There is always hope.

When we see a child's sleep issues and the effect they are having as warning signals that something is going on in the child's life instead of pathologizing them, we can reconceptualize the way we see sleep *and* reduce the child's stress surrounding sleep. Additionally, as we work through the Neurocycle process with our children in other areas of life, we may even find this will end up helping them with their sleep struggles, as we saw in Tim's story. Everything is connected.

Nightmares

People can have nightmares at any age, but they appear to be very common in children ages 3–12.[24] Although the exact cause of nightmares is not fully understood, there are several reasons children may have them. Dreams occur during rapid eye movement (REM) sleep. We start with non-REM sleep (NREM), where the mind and brain stop processing the outside world, then progress into REM sleep, where the mind and brain start processing our inner thought life.[25]

As we saw in part 1, thoughts, with their embedded memories, are stored in three places: the mind, the brain, and the body. The emotions that are tangled up with the data of these thoughts can create an imbalance in and a disruption to the homeostasis of the mind, brain, and body if they are toxic or unmanaged. Nightmares potentially arise from this tangled web, which can be caused by chronic issues such as trauma or by day-to-day issues such as fighting with a sibling.[26]

When we are asleep, the nonconscious mind steps in to sort out these imbalances, trying to restore order to our thinking. Nightmares seem to be one way the mind tries to make sense of our experiences. Brain scans show that the part of the brain that is highly active when the mind processes emotional perceptions, the amygdala (or "library"), becomes almost frantic when we have a nightmare; it's as though the mind is dealing with a toxic imbalance.[27] However, the part of the brain that responds to balance the amygdala, the prefrontal cortex (PFC), is less active. As a result, toxic blocks or suppressed thoughts and traumas may be hidden from the conscious mind and only come out when we are asleep. This is why responding to the patterns in our dreams as warning signals and messengers, or becoming what I call a "thought dream detective," is an important skill to teach our children.

Dreams and nightmares will be unique to every child.[28] Generally, their own perspectives, imagination, and creativity will be expressed in both their dreams and their nightmares. As you work through the Neurocycle process with your child, you will start to notice patterns of stressors in their life, and you may then be able to connect them with their dreams.

23

Sleep Issues and the Neurocycle

There is no magic number of hours that a child needs to sleep every night. Observe your child, see how they respond to different sleep schedules, and take the time to find out what works best for them.

Helping your child prepare for sleep begins in the morning, as counterintuitive as this may sound. The way their mind is managed from the time they wake up impacts their biochemistry, their circadian rhythm, and the energy flow in their conscious mind and brain.[1] These, in turn, will impact how the rest of their day *and* night go.

An unmanaged, messy mind and brain can result in a messy day and a messy night (i.e., sleep disturbances). This is why I recommend you do what I call a "waking-up sleep Neurocycle," which I discuss below, to help your child set a healthy daily routine. This is a quick and easy process and can be done in a couple of minutes. You can even include the whole family in this routine if you wish.

If sleep is an issue for your child, or if they have a pattern of sleep problems, in addition to the waking-up sleep Neurocycle, strive to also do a full 63-day Neurocycle to try to unearth the

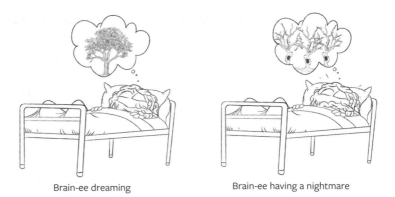

Brain-ee dreaming

Brain-ee having a nightmare

potential thought trees that are affecting your child's sleep, which I also discuss below. A few Neurocycles may be needed, because repeated and persistent nightmares are an indication something is trying to come out from the nonconscious mind.[2]

The Neurocycle can also be used as a tool alongside seeking professional help for your child, if needed. As you work through this process with your child, you will be helping them unwire and rewire the neural networks of their brain—making those unhealthy thought trees into healthy, blossoming thought trees. This, in turn, will help calm down their HPA axis, increasing their ability to fall asleep and sleep well.

Waking-Up Sleep Neurocycle

You can make the waking-up sleep Neurocycle a fun little routine you do as you hug and kiss your child awake. You may find you can run through all 5 Steps while they are still in bed, or you may need to do this while you get them up and ready. At first this may feel clumsy, but once you have done it a few times, it will get easier and will eventually become a routine you can probably do in under a minute.

Remember, you are helping teach your child to be observant about themselves and start self-regulating as they wake up, which, as mentioned above, is an excellent way to improve brain health and prepare them for sleep at night. This is also a great way to connect with your child at the start of the day and to get to know them on a deeper level. Your child will feel you are tuning in to them, which helps create a safe space where they can be open with you and talk to you.

1. Gather Awareness

Help your child Gather Awareness of their four warning signals by gently prompting them with some questions as they wake up and/or while you are getting them ready for the day. These warning signals are related to how they are waking up and how they slept.

For all ages—using words, pictures, or toys as appropriate—ask your child things like:

"Are you happy? Sad? Worried? Excited?"

"How do you feel in your body? Does anything feel sore or uncomfortable?" (You can point to different parts of the body as you do this to help them communicate how they feel.)

While you are asking them questions, take note of their perspective and attitude as they wake up. Are they complaining? Are they happy or excited? Also ask them questions about how they feel about the day to come or how they feel about how they slept last night.

2. Reflect

Transition quickly into the Reflect step with a simple question: "Why do you feel like this?" They may not say much because they are still sleepy, so you may have to provide words, toys, or pictures as prompts.

While you are doing this, do you notice a thought that these four signals are perhaps attached to? Is this a consistent pattern in your child's life or a one-off situation?

If your child had a dream or nightmare they want to talk about, remember that dreams and nightmares aren't clear-cut explanations or signals but rather products of the sorting process done by the nonconscious mind to clean up the brain in preparation for the next day—kind of like housekeeping. You are not trying to interpret their dreams or nightmares; you are just trying to observe the kinds of speech, body movements, emotions, and attitudes they are producing in your child, and if there are any consistent themes.

It is also important to remember that not every child will recall their dreams, and that's totally fine. Just the process of going through these steps will give you insight into your child's mood and is an excellent way to teach them to practice daily self-regulation. Even if there is very little response from your child at first, and you are doing most of the talking while they just nod or shake their head, something is still going on in their mind and brain—even if it seems nothing is happening.

For all ages—using words, pictures, or toys as appropriate—ask your child things like:

"Why do you feel sad, happy, cross, or ____?"

"Why do you think you feel like this?"

"Do you want to show me what you feel like using your toys or pictures [such as the Brain-ee toy or pictures of Brain-ee]?"

3. Write/Play/Draw

Because this waking-up sleep Neurocycle should take only a few minutes, you don't actually have to tell your child to write or draw how they feel and why. You can help them visualize this step by getting them to imagine and describe how they feel and why they think they feel this way.

For Ages 3–5

You can have your boxes of pictures on hand (the four signals boxes and the Reflect box) in case they want to grab one as you help them visualize this step. I also recommend having a pen and paper ready just in case you or they want to draw something. Sometimes your child may be too distressed or too tired to talk and may find drawing a helpful way to communicate.

You can ask something like:

"Do you want to show me a picture about your dream?"
"Can you tell me about what you dreamed?"

As you do this step, you can also point to the picture of Brain-ee sleeping with dreams and thoughts coming out of his brain at the beginning of this chapter, and you can tell your child, "We need to catch these sleeping thoughts going through your brain and try to mend them, because they may affect how you sleep." You can then ask them if they had a dream like Brain-ee's and ask them to explain it to you as much as they can.

For Ages 6–10

For this step, you can ask your child questions similar to those for the younger age group but include more words. You can ask them something like, "Do you need me to help you with some words to help explain how you feel?"

4. Recheck

For the Recheck step, you can take what your child told you in Steps 1–3 and look for patterns. Your child can work through this process by reviewing what they visualized in Step 3 and add to it. If your child was too tired or didn't say anything, you can, based on your observations of their state of mind, give them an encouraging and loving statement they can remember for the day so they feel loved and safe, which will help calm down their stress response and increase the likelihood they will sleep well the next night.

For Ages 3–5

For your child age 3–5, you can say something like:

"I'm here for you to always help you. Can I hug you to make you feel better?" (Use this step only if they like hugs.)

"I am so proud of how brave you are for telling me about your dream or nightmare. Let's think of a nice dream for tonight. What would you like to dream about?"

"You will be doing so many fun things today that will help you feel better! Let's list a few of these fun things."

"I know ＿＿＿ is bothering you and affected how you slept last night. Remember, you don't have to figure everything out and make it all better today. Let's do ＿＿＿ to try to make it a bit better, yes?"

For Ages 6–10

For your child age 6–10, you can say something like the statements above or be more descriptive with your words. For example, if your child is fighting with their friend, you can say something like, "I know you don't know how to fix the fight you had with your friend, but you don't have to figure out everything today. How about you take this cookie (or treat or gift) to give to them and see how they respond? This may make things better, and then you will have better dreams tonight!" Or, if your child feels like their friends make fun of them and are making them have nightmares, you can say something like, "I know your friends say they think you are weird and make fun of you a lot, but you are not weird. You are unique and amazing! You have a unique thinking superpower, like Brain-ee [show them the superhero picture again, if you want].

Today, try to practice loving yourself instead of worrying about what other people think of you. When you feel sad, remember what I said to you this morning: you are amazing!"

5. Active Reach

Help your child craft a statement they can practice throughout the day that is solution oriented, perhaps using your words from Step 4. Remind your child to practice their Active Reach to help them feel better throughout the day and sleep better at night.

For Ages 3–5

Help your child age 3–5 draw a picture to remind them of their Active Reach for that day. You can also give them a sticker or toy to remind them—make sure this is something they can take to school as well if you are not with them during the day.

For Ages 6–10

You can use the suggestions above for ages 3–5 if you wish, or if your child has a device, you can help them set their own reminders for practicing their Active Reach.

A Sleep Issue Neurocycle

As mentioned above, if sleep is an issue for your child, or if they have a pattern of sleep problems, do the Neurocycle below over 63 days to try to unearth the potential thought trees and issues that are affecting your child's sleep.

1. Gather Awareness

Gather Awareness of whether your child is displaying a sleep pattern that is different from usual and how this is showing up in their emotional, behavioral, bodily sensation, and perspective warning signals. You can use the examples in the waking-up sleep Neurocycle above. Do this as early in the day as possible.

2. Reflect

As you Reflect on what you Gathered Awareness of with your child in Step 1, do a quick self-check. How are you seeing your child? Are your own experiences with sleep impacting how you see and understand what your child is going through? Are you really trying to tune in to what your child is experiencing?

Comparing their sleep patterns to your experiences or the experiences of another family member may make you think that what they are doing is a problem because it is or isn't the same. We should always try to contextualize our children's experiences in real time based on their unique context, staying as free as possible from our own biases. Otherwise, we may be at risk of having a skewed perspective, which can make things more stressful for everyone involved.

When a child seems to be acting out and refusing to sleep, they may be expressing frustration toward something that is upsetting or confusing them and trying to communicate this to you.

When a child seems to be acting out and refusing to sleep, they may be expressing frustration toward something that is upsetting or confusing them and trying to communicate this to you. It is important to reflect on what is *behind* their specific warning signals, not just to discipline them away. We need to help our children see what thoughts these warning signals are attached to over time, which pulls up the memories clustered into the thought so that your child can work on reconceptualizing the thought tree(s) and changing their behavior (as discussed in parts 1 and 2).

I love how Tim explained this to me. He said his different dreams and nightmares were "like oceans and catching fish in the sea. Sometimes the dreams are so scary. It's like the dark ocean is full of sharks that are very scary, and I need lots of help from my mom and dad to help me kill one of these sharks. But sometimes the dreams are little dreams, like just catching little fishes that don't make me feel bad, just excited about catching a fish so I can take it home and take care of it. And sometimes, the dreams are so nice it's like watching dolphins swim all around you, which makes me feel so happy."

You can use this example if you wish to help your child understand what dreams and nightmares are like and why you are doing the Neurocycle together to help them. You can also use the thought tree imagery discussed below to help them understand.

For Ages 3–5

You can explain to your child age 3–5 that their bad dreams or night sweats (or whatever the issue is) are like "little hurts" in their brain or broken leaves and branches on their thought trees. When they talk about them using pictures, words, or toys, they are helping get to the root of these thought trees to make them better and healthy so that they are not scared of sleeping anymore. You can use the image of Brain-ee enjoying his healthy thought tree development in chapter 15 to help with this.

For Ages 6–10

You can explain Tim's fishing analogy or the thought tree imagery above, or you can help your child make up their own analogy. Remind them how the thought trees they are looking at with their broken branches (the warning signals) are getting weaker just because they are talking about them—they aren't hiding in the ground (nonconscious mind) doing harm. They are coming out into the open so that your child can make them healthy.

3. Write/Play/Draw

In this step, help your child draw, enact with toys, use pictures, write, or visualize whatever you discussed in the Gather Awareness and Reflect steps above.

For Ages 3–5

As you do Step 3 with your child age 3–5, you can ask questions and make statements based on the sleep issue they are having, such as:

"What was your bad dream about? Can you show me what your dream was about using pictures or your toys?"

"It's okay; you are safe now. I am right here with you."

"You don't have to tell me now; we can talk about this later."

"Let's write/play/draw about your dream in another room so we take the scary stuff away from your bedroom."

For Ages 6–10

For your child age 6–10, you can use the statements and questions above based on the sleep issue they are having. You can also have your child follow Tim's example. He made a dream Neurocycle sheet with his mom to help him sleep better, which you also may find helpful with your child. He completed this sheet to use in his Recheck and Active Reach steps. On the sheet are statements similar to the following, with spaces to draw and write:

1. I didn't like what I dreamed about last night because it made me feel . . .
2. Here are the things I wish didn't happen . . .
3. Here is a picture changing the ending to one I would like.
4. I can change my dream because . . .

I didn't like my dream last night. Here are things that I wish didn't happen and want to change:

- _____
- _____
- _____
- _____
- _____

Draw a picture changing the ending of your dream to one you would like. You can choose any ending!

I can change my dream because I am stronger than it. I can change my dream because...
I can change...

Tim's sleep Neurocycle sheet

4. Recheck

There may be lots of memories clustered into thought trees popping up into your child's conscious awareness that are associated with their sleep issue. The key to helping your child in this step is to try to put the pieces together for them slowly over time, based on how much they can handle. Take what you did in Steps 1–3 and help them craft a statement they can practice throughout the day that is solution oriented.

Remember to use the decompression exercises in chapter 7 to help your child if they are starting to feel stressed or upset.

For Ages 3–5

In this step, let your child explain and talk about what they wrote, drew, acted out, or visualized in Step 3. This will help them feel more in control over what doesn't make sense to them and help them find ways they can practice making things better (or reconceptualizing and making that thought tree healthy).

Just being with them and listening in order to solve this sleep issue together helps build a collaborative and facilitative relationship with your child instead of you just trying to fix their issue or labeling them.

For Ages 6–10

Tim showed me a picture he had drawn of a house with two chimneys that represented his sleep house. One chimney had black smoke (the scary nightmares) and one had light smoke (the nice dreams). He explained that as he Rechecked the nightmare using the Neurocycle, he decided to burn the bad story (dark smoke) and replace it with a nice story (light smoke), and that is what he would practice thinking about when he went to sleep that night. He then said he was going to work on the stories of what the nightmares meant with his mom and dad because he thought they were telling him more about what happened to him when he was little. He would then create a new version of the story that made him feel better, less angry, and more at peace during the 63 days of his next Neurocycle.

You can do something like this with your child. They can come up with their own sleep image, or you can use the pictures of the toxic tree (see part 1). Keep this step as simple and easy to remember and apply as possible, like Tim thinking of his chimney image before sleeping and telling himself that he is going to find out what the dreams are telling him to make his story better—or make his thought trees healthy. Be as comforting and supportive as possible as you do this with your child, saying something like, "I am so sorry for how this made you feel. Let's work on making this better together."

During this step, you can also tell your child how you dealt with something that frightened you and made you have nightmares, or what you do when you have a bad dream. For example, you can say something like, "When I have a bad dream and wake up, I always sit up in bed and tell myself this isn't true and that I can find out what it means tomorrow when I'm awake. Right now, I am safe in bed. Then I turn the light on and think of something happy or read or watch something funny until I am calm and tired again." This can help your child think of some ideas of their own, or they can use your ideas to come up with their Active Reach to practice the new, healthy thought tree they are trying to grow.

5. Active Reach

Choose one of the statements from the Recheck step you and your child came up with and encourage your child to write or draw a picture to remind them of this throughout the day (you can also help them draw or write this). For example, Tim chose his Active Reach from his sleep Neurocycle sheet and set an alarm on his watch to go off seven times during the day to remind himself to practice his Active Reach.

Below are some great Active Reaches you can do with your child of any age to help them manage their sleep issue:

- Help your child craft a statement that helps them practice feeling safe and at peace when they go to sleep, such as "I am safe. My family is here to make sure I am safe."
- Encourage your child to hug their favorite toy or Brain-ee toy when they go to sleep to remind them that their mind is strong and that they are stronger than the nightmare or other sleep issue.
- Encourage your child to draw a picture of the scary dream or their sleep issue and then fold it up and put it in a box they can close or lock, then reopen when they are ready during the day to do the Neurocycle about the issue with you. Remind them that they don't have to make everything better right now. They have time, and things will improve.
- Make their room feel like a safe and fun place. Play games in their room, put drawings all over the walls, build a makeshift

tent filled with everything they love and let them sleep in it, play their favorite music, or do something else that will make where they sleep a nice and happy place to be. Do this with your child so they feel like they are doing something positive and constructive to make the situation better.

- Reward and praise your child as soon as they wake up in the morning for being brave enough to sleep and knowing that their bedroom is a safe place. At the same time, remind them they can always talk to you when they feel scared or worried.
- Read a happy story to your child before bed and get them to close their eyes and imagine what they are hearing. This will help them fall asleep with happy thoughts and images in their head.

Additional Tips for Helping Your Child through Sleep and Nightmare Challenges

Below are some additional tips you may find helpful as you work through the Neurocycle with your child to help them overcome any sleep and nightmare challenges. These also make great Active Reach prompts.

- Remember that there is no magic number of hours that a child needs to sleep every night. Observe your child, see how they respond to different sleep schedules, and take the time to find out what works best for them. Some people may need more sleep than others, so don't compare your child's sleep patterns to those of their siblings or other children.
- Some children may find that certain tips to improve sleep quality don't work for them—this is perfectly okay *and* normal. Experiment and see what works best for your child.
- If your child is experiencing sleep disturbances, try first to see what they are going through within the context of their

unique experiences. What is going on in their life that may be impacting their sleep? Have there been any major changes in their life recently? You could observe this over a few days or even weeks.

- See a sleep therapist or professional if the sleep disturbances get worse or continue over an extended period of time. Never be ashamed of asking for help. Sleep issues can be related to a biological or neurological issue, so they are worth investigating.

Conclusion

The science of neuroplasticity shows us that we can help our children heal, repair, and grow. The challenges of life don't have to lead to permanent damage in their mind, brain, or body.

As a parent or caregiver, you need to know that negative, fearful thoughts actually change your child's brain structure and chemistry, as mentioned in part 1. When this happens in a young, developing brain, its impact can carry over into adolescence and adulthood.

There is an extensive body of research about the impact of adverse childhood experiences on the mind, brain, body, mental health, and future of children, much of which has been cited throughout this book. As mentioned before, excessive levels of unmanaged stress and toxic thoughts in children can result in a greater susceptibility to physical illness and long-term mental health issues. We cannot overlook the impact our children's mental health has on their life.

However, it's incredibly important to focus on the fact that there is so much hope. The science of neuroplasticity shows us that we can help our children heal, repair, and grow. The challenges of life don't have to lead to permanent damage in their mind, brain, or body. Through mind-management, your child can learn how to take control of their life. You can teach your child how to write their own stories.

This doesn't mean erasing what has happened to our children or protecting them from everything that can harm them. As much as we may want to do this, it's impossible. As I have pointed out throughout this book, we will never be able to change what has happened to our children, but we can change how what happens to them looks inside their mind, brain, and body and how their experiences play out in their future. This is mind-management in action.

Through mind-management, your child can learn how to take control of their life. You can teach your child how to write their own stories.

We can teach our children that life isn't just about trying to eliminate troubling thoughts. It's about cleaning up those mental messes we will inevitably experience as human beings. This means helping our children get to the *why* behind their thoughts and how these thoughts are showing up in their life. Then we can help them come to accept and find peace in what has happened.

In this book, you have been learning how to do this with your child through the Neurocycle. This whole system is designed to help our children accept and shape their own unique stories. As we do this, we help our children learn to embrace all their humanity; develop their self-regulatory skills, autonomy, and identity; build up their resilience; increase their confidence; and manage stress and anxiety. This is the foundation of mental well-being. We are teaching our children how to be mental health superheroes, just like Brain-ee!

Acknowledgments

I acknowledge every researcher, scientist, philosopher, and teacher I've ever read and learned from, because it's on the shoulders of giants that we make little steps forward into the future to make the necessary changes that help to repair and heal humanity.

I acknowledge my three phenomenal daughters, whom I am so privileged to have work full-time with me. Alexy, my youngest daughter and my research assistant, spent literally hours by my side, talking through and helping me map out and make sense of endless ideas and research in this enormous field. She meticulously screened my every word for clarity and scientific accuracy. Her insight was phenomenal, wise, and invaluable. Jessica, my eldest daughter, heads our customer and app technical support, newsletter, and blog and is incredibly efficient at everything she does. She brilliantly edited and shaped my somewhat clinical and scientific way of writing into an easy to understand flow that even I get excited reading. Dominique, my second eldest daughter, remarkable podcast producer, and marketing and business development head, has an exceptional way of guiding concept formation throughout all projects, including the book development process, and is fantastic at seeing the key points in the final manuscript that need to be emphasized, helping pull it into a cohesive whole.

I acknowledge Gabby, who is on my research team and who did an outstanding job helping with the layout and getting the endless references updated and into the right order and format—a laborious task that requires an eye for detail. She did an amazing job.

I acknowledge Tim (his pseudonym) and his stepmom and dad for allowing me the honor of interweaving their very moving story into my book. It's not easy being vulnerable, but they were, and I know that as you read their story, you will be helped and feel hope in so many ways.

I acknowledge Brian, my editor at Baker Books, for his ability to stand back and observe the big picture and give input that always improves the flow of the manuscript. I also acknowledge the rest of the Baker team, with whom I have been working since 2013. You are kind and fun and always so professional and encouraging.

I acknowledge my son, Jeffrey, who is a great storyteller and writer and is coauthoring children's storybooks about the adventures of Brain-ee, who you have met throughout this book, being transported to a mysterious place called the quantum realm, where he learns how to use an ancient superpower, the Neurocycle, and faces and conquers the toxic thought monster that threatens to take over the minds of everyone and destroy the world. You will be able to read these stories alongside Neurocycling with your children to help them manage their mental health.

I acknowledge my mom, Anne, my biggest fan, who has taught me so much about parenting.

Twenty-five years ago, I dreamed up the Brain-ee character you see in this book. Saraia, my illustrator, has done an exceptionally fabulous job updating twenty-five-year-old Brain-ee and taking my visions of Brain-ee to a whole new level in this book, helping to take you and your children on a journey to manage your collective mental health.

I acknowledge all my patients over the years who have helped me see challenge and pain and healing through their eyes—an extreme privilege I don't take lightly and honor with all my ongoing research to make mental health accessible to everyone.

I, of course, cannot *not* acknowledge Simba and Nala, my shih tzus, for making me laugh and cuddling and comforting me through the long hours it takes to write a book.

And last but not least, I acknowledge my husband, Mac, who is the CEO of our company. His support is endless, from breakfast in bed when I have burned the midnight oil to a never-ending supply of unconditional support and love in every way possible. I am strong, Mac, because you believe in me and my work. I love you endlessly.

Notes

Preface

1. "The State of Mental Health in America," Mental Health America, accessed August 25, 2022, https://www.mhanational.org/issues/state-mental-health-america.
2. "U.S. Surgeon General Issues Advisory on Youth Mental Health Crisis Further Exposed by COVID-19 Pandemic," U.S. Department of Health & Human Services, December 7, 2021, https://www.hhs.gov/about/news/2021/12/07/us-surgeon-general-issues-advisory-on -youth-mental-health-crisis-further-exposed-by-covid-19-pandemic.html.
3. Mental Health Million Project, "Mental State of the World 2021," Sapien Labs, accessed August 25, 2022, https://sapienlabs.org/wp-content/uploads/2022/03/Mental-State -of-the-World-Report-2021.pdf.
4. "Stress Effects on the Body," American Psychological Association, November 1, 2018, https://www.apa.org/topics/stress/body.
5. Rae Jacobson, "Metacognition: How Thinking About Thinking Can Help Kids," Child Mind Institute, August 15, 2021, https://childmind.org/article/how-metacognition -can-help-kids/.

Chapter 1 The Mind-Brain-Body Connection

1. Ralph Lewis, "What Actually Is a Thought and How Is Information Physical?," *Psychology Today*, February 24, 2019, https://www.psychologytoday.com/us/blog/finding -purpose/201902/what-actually-is-thought-and-how-is-information-physical.
2. Arlin Cuncic, "What Happens to Your Body When You're Thinking?," VeryWellMind, July 17, 2019, https://www.verywellmind.com/what-happens-when-you-think-4688619.
3. "Mental Illness and the Family: Recognizing Warning Signs and How to Cope," Mental Health America, accessed August 25, 2022, https://www.mhanational.org/recog nizing-warning-signs.
4. Kendra Cherry, "What Is Neuroplasticity?," VeryWellMind, February 18, 2022, https://www.verywellmind.com/what-is-brain-plasticity-2794886.
5. Giorgio A. Ascoli, *Trees of the Brain, Roots of the Mind* (Cambridge, MA: MIT Press, 2015).
6. Danielle Pacheco and Heather Write, "How Do Dreams Affect Sleep?," Sleep Foundation, March 18, 2022, https://www.sleepfoundation.org/dreams/how-do-dreams-affect -sleep.

7. Zamzuri Idris, "Quantum Physics Perspective on Electromagnetic and Quantum Fields Inside the Brain," *Malaysian Journal of Medical Sciences* 27, no. 1 (2020): 1–5, https://www.ncbi.nlm.nih.gov/pmc/articles/PMC7053547/.

8. Caroline Leaf et al., "The Development of a Model for Geodesic Learning: The Geodesic Information Processing Model," *The South African Journal of Communication Disorders* 44 (1997): 53–77. For more information, see Caroline Leaf, *Think, Learn, Succeed: Understanding and Using Your Mind to Thrive at School, the Workplace, and Life* (Grand Rapids: Baker Books, 2018), chap. 22.

9. Emma Young, "Lifting the Lid on the Unconscious," *New Scientist*, July 25, 2018, https://www.newscientist.com/article/mg23931880-400-lifting-the-lid-on-the-unconscious/; Leaf et al., "The Development of a Model for Geodesic Learning."

10. Matt James, "Conscious of the Unconscious," *Psychology Today*, July 30, 2013, https://www.psychologytoday.com/us/blog/focus-forgiveness/201307/conscious-the-unconscious.

11. Caroline Leaf, "Why Mind-Management Is the Solution to Cleaning Up Your Mental Mess: White Paper," accessed September 13, 2022, https://cdn.shopify.com/s/files/1/1810/9163/files/General_White_Paper_100720_final_version.pdf?v=1602124109.

12. Greg Lukianoff and Jonathan Haidt, *The Coddling of the American Mind: How Good Intentions and Bad Ideas Are Setting Up a Generation for Failure* (New York: Penguin, 2018), 24.

13. Nassim Nicholas Taleb, *Antifragile: Things That Gain from Disorder* (New York: Random House, 2012).

Chapter 5 Helpful Guidelines

1. Raising Children Network, "3–4 Years: Preschooler Development," Raising Children: The Australian Parenting Website, accessed December 13, 2022, https://raisingchildren.net.au/preschoolers/development/development-tracker/3-4-years; ACT, "Cognitive and Social Skills to Expect from 3 to 5 Years," American Psychological Association, accessed December 13, 2022, https://www.apa.org/act/resources/fact-sheets/development-5-years.

2. Grupo MContigo, "From the Subconscious Mind to the Conscious Mind," *Exploring Your Mind* (blog), December 9, 2017, https://exploringyourmind.com/subconscious-mind-conscious-mind/.

3. Raising Children Network, "5–6 Years: Preschooler Development," Raising Children: The Australian Parenting Website, accessed December 13, 2022, https://raisingchildren.net.au/school-age/development/development-tracker/5-6-years; Wendy Wisner, "5-Year-Old Child Development Milestones," VeryWellFamily, February 3, 2022, https://www.verywellfamily.com/5-year-old-developmental-milestones-620713.

4. Raising Children Network, "6–8 Years: Child Development," Raising Children: The Australian Parenting Website, accessed December 13, 2022, https://raisingchildren.net.au/school-age/development/development-tracker/6-8-years; Wendy Wisner, "7-Year-Old Child Development Milestones," VeryWellFamily, March 15, 2022, https://www.verywellfamily.com/7-year-old-developmental-milestones-620704.

5. Elisa Cinelli, "9-Year-Old Child Development Milestones," VeryWellFamily, March 14, 2022, https://www.verywellfamily.com/9-year-old-developmental-milestones-620731; Centers for Disease Control and Prevention, "Middle Childhood (9–11 Years of Age)," CDC Child Development, September 23, 2021, https://www.cdc.gov/ncbddd/childdevelopment/positiveparenting/middle2.html.

Chapter 6 The Power of Self-Regulation

1. Marianne Stein, "When Mom and Child Interact, Physiology and Behavior Coordinate," ScienceDaily, November 11, 2021, https://www.sciencedaily.com/releases/2021/11/211111130301.htm.

Chapter 8 How to Do Step 1: Gather Awareness

1. New York University, "Young Children's Sense of Self Is Similar to That of Adults," ScienceDaily, August 24, 2017, https://www.sciencedaily.com/releases/2017/08/170824110614.htm.

Chapter 12 How to Do Step 5: Active Reach

1. I. G. Sarason, "Anxiety, Self-Preoccupation and Attention," *Anxiety Research* 1, no. 1 (1988): 3–7.

Chapter 13 The Timing of the Neurocycle

1. Srini Pillay, "Your Brain Can Only Take So Much Focus," *Harvard Business Review*, May 12, 2017, https://hbr.org/2017/05/your-brain-can-only-take-so-much-focus; Megan Reitz and Michael Chaskalson, "Mindfulness Works but Only If You Work at It," *Harvard Business Review*, November 4, 2016, https://hbr.org/2016/11/mindfulness-works-but-only-if-you-work-at-it?registration=success.

2. Emily Swaim, "7 Reminders to Carry with You on Your Trauma Recovery Journey," Healthline, May 25, 2022, https://www.healthline.com/health/mental-health/trauma-recovery.

3. Ben D. Gardner, "Busting the 21 Days Habit Formation Myth," *Health Chatter* (blog), June 29, 2012, https://blogs.ucl.ac.uk/bsh/2012/06/29/busting-the-21-days-habit-formation-myth/.

4. Society for Personality and Social Psychology, "How We Form Habits, Change Existing Ones," ScienceDaily, August 8, 2014, https://www.sciencedaily.com/releases/2014/08/140808111931.htm. See also Caroline Leaf, *Cleaning Up Your Mental Mess: 5 Simple, Scientifically Proven Steps to Reduce Anxiety, Stress, and Toxic Thinking* (Grand Rapids: Baker Books, 2021), chap. 10.

5. Lou Whitaker, "How Does Thinking Positive Thoughts Affect Neuroplasticity?," Meteor Education, accessed September 14, 2022, https://meteoreducation.com/how-does-thinking-positive-thoughts-affect-neuroplasticity/.

6. Courtney E. Ackerman, "23 Amazing Health Benefits of Mindfulness for Body and Brain," *Positive Psychology* (blog), March 6, 2017, https://positivepsychology.com/benefits-of-mindfulness/.

7. Jerry Fodor, "Précis of *The Modularity of Mind*," *Behavioral and Brain Sciences* 8 (1985): 1–42, https://media.pluto.psy.uconn.edu/Fodor%20modularity%20precis%20w%20comment.pdf.

8. Eddie Harmon-Jones, Philip A. Gable, and Tom F. Price, "The Influence of Affective States Varying in Motivational Intensity on Cognitive Scope," *Frontiers in Integrative Neuroscience* 6 (September 10, 2012): 73, https://www.ncbi.nlm.nih.gov/pmc/articles/PMC3437552/.

Chapter 14 Trauma

1. "Complex Trauma: Effects," The National Child Traumatic Stress Network, accessed September 14, 2022, https://www.nctsn.org/what-is-child-trauma/trauma-types/complex-trauma/effects.

2. Jasmine Purnomo, "Wired for Danger: The Effects of Childhood Trauma on the Brain," BrainFacts, October 19, 2020, https://www.brainfacts.org/thinking-sensing-and-behaving/childhood-and-adolescence/2020/wired-for-danger-the-effects-of-childhood-trauma-on-the-brain-101920.

3. Nathan H. Lents, "Trauma, PTSD, and Memory Distortion," *Psychology Today*, May 23, 2016, https://www.psychologytoday.com/us/blog/beastly-behavior/201605/trauma-ptsd-and-memory-distortion.

4. Neuroscience Center, "The Brain and Common Psychiatric Disorders," *Psychology Today*, accessed September 14, 2022, https://www.psychologytoday.com/us/basics/neuroscience/the-brain-and-common-psychiatric-disorders.

5. Erin Maynard, "How Trauma and PTSD Impact the Brain," VeryWellMind, February 13, 2020, https://www.verywellmind.com/what-exactly-does-ptsd-do-to-the-brain-2797210.

6. David Waters, "Memphis Scientists Treat Young Trauma Victims by 'Training' Their Brain Waves," The Institute for Public Service Reporting Memphis, September 13, 2019, https://www.psrmemphis.org/part-2-memphis-scientists-treat-young-trauma-victims-by-training-their-brain-waves.

7. Leigh G. Goetchius et al., "Amygdala-Prefrontal Cortex White Matter Tracts Are Widespread, Variable and Implicated in Amygdala Modulation in Adolescents," *Neuroimage* 191 (2019), https://www.ncbi.nlm.nih.gov/pmc/articles/PMC6440813/.

8. Leaf, "Why Mind-Management Is the Solution."

9. Min Jin Jin et al., "An Integrated Model of Emotional Problems, Beta Power of Electroencephalography, and Low Frequency of Heart Rate Variability after Childhood Trauma in a Non-Clinical Sample: A Path Analysis Study," *Psychiatry* 8 (January 22, 2018), https://www.frontiersin.org/articles/10.3389/fpsyt.2017.00314/full.

10. Children's Welfare Information Gateway, "Parenting a Child Who Has Experienced Trauma," *Fact Sheet for Families*, November 2014, https://www.childwelfare.gov/pubpdfs/child-trauma.pdf.

11. Leah K. Gilbert et al., "Childhood Adversity and Adult Chronic Disease: An Update from Ten States and the District of Columbia," *American Journal of Preventive Medicine* 48, no. 3 (March 1, 2015): 345–49, https://doi.org/10.1016/j.amepre.2014.09.006.

12. Rachel A. Vaughn-Coaxum et al., "Associations between Trauma Type, Timing, and Accumulation on Current Coping Behaviors in Adolescents: Results from a Large, Population-Based Sample," *Journal of Youth and Adolescence* 47 (2018): 842–58, https://doi.org/10.1007%2Fs10964-017-0693-5.

13. Leaf, "Why Mind-Management Is the Solution."

Chapter 16 Identity Issues

1. University of Zurich, "Every Person Has a Unique Brain Anatomy," ScienceDaily, July 10, 2018, https://www.sciencedaily.com/releases/2018/07/180710104631.htm.

2. Johanna Kehusmaa et al., "The Association between the Social Environment of Childhood and Adolescence and Depression in Young Adulthood: A Prospective Cohort Study," *Journal of Affective Disorders* 305 (May 15, 2022): 37–46, https://www.sciencedirect.com/science/article/pii/S0165032722002166#s0090/.

3. Bob Cunningham, "The Importance of Positive Self-Esteem for Kids," Understood, accessed September 14, 2022, https://www.understood.org/en/articles/the-importance-of-positive-self-esteem-for-kids.

4. Lauren DiMaria, "The Importance of a Child's Social Identity," VeryWellMind, April 25, 2022, https://www.verywellmind.com/the-importance-of-a-childs-social-identity-1066758.

5. John Sciamanna, "Increased Suicide Rates among Children Aged 5 to 11 Years in the U.S.," Child Welfare League of America, accessed September 14, 2022, https://www.cwla.org/increased-suicide-rates-among-children-aged-5-to-11-years-in-the-u-s/.

6. Peter Sterling and Simon Laughlin, *Principles of Neural Design* (Cambridge, MA: MIT Press, 2015).

7. Journal of the American Medical Association, "Levels of Certain Hormones May Be Increased by Stress," ScienceDaily, August 3, 2004, https://www.sciencedaily.com/releases/2004/08/040803094422.htm.

8. Paul Fitzgerald and Brendon Watson, "Gamma Oscillations as a Biomarker for Major Depression: An Emerging Topic," *Translational Psychiatry* 8, article 177 (September 4, 2018), https://www.nature.com/articles/s41398-018-0239-y; Sang-Choong Roh et al., "EEG Beta and Low Gamma Power Correlates with Inattention in Patients with Major Depressive Disorder," *Journal of Affective Disorders* 204 (November 1, 2016): 124–30, http://dx.doi.org/10.1016/j.jad.2016.06.033.

9. Jaskanwal Deep Singh Sara et al., "Mental Stress and Its Effects on Vascular Health," *Mayo Clinic Proceedings* 97, no. 5 (May 1, 2022): 951–90, https://www.mayoclinicproceedings.org/article/S0025-6196(22)00104-5/fulltext; Jiongjiong Wang et al., "Perfusion Functional MRI Reveals Cerebral Blood Flow Pattern under Psychological Stress," *Proceedings of the National Academy of Sciences of the United States of America* 102, no. 49 (November 23, 2005): 17804–9, https://doi.org/10.1073%2Fpnas.0503082102.

10. Rammohan V. Rao and Dale E. Bredesen, "Misfolded Proteins, Endoplasmic Reticulum Stress and Neurodegeneration," *Current Opinions in Cellular Biology* 16, no. 6 (December 2004): 653–62, https://www.ncbi.nlm.nih.gov/pmc/articles/PMC3970707/.

11. Fulvio D'Acquisto, "Affective Immunology: Where Emotions and the Immune Response Converge," *Dialogues in Clinical Neuroscience* 19, no. 1 (March 2017): 9–19, https://www.ncbi.nlm.nih.gov/pmc/articles/PMC5442367/.

12. Asuka Sawai et al., "Influence of Mental Stress on the Plasma Homocysteine Level and Blood Pressure Change in Young Men," *Clinical and Experimental Hypertension* 30, no. 3 (2008): 233–41, https://doi.org/10.1080/10641960802068725.

13. Elizabeth Blackburn and Elissa Epel, *The Telomere Effect: A Revolutionary Approach to Living Younger, Healthier, Longer* (New York: Grand Central, 2017).

14. Walaa Elsayed, "The Negative Effects of Social Media on the Social Identity of Adolescents from the Perspective of Social Work," *Heliyon* 7, no. 2 (February 2021), https://www.sciencedirect.com/science/article/pii/S2405844021004321.

15. Eva Lazar, "How Parents Can Foster Autonomy and Encourage Child Development," *Good Therapy* (blog), July 4, 2018, https://www.goodtherapy.org/blog/how-parents-can-foster-autonomy-encourage-child-development-0704184.

16. Kendra Cherry, "Why Parenting Styles Matter When Raising Children," VeryWellMind, April 14, 2020, https://www.verywellmind.com/parenting-styles-2795072.

17. Rae Jacobson, "Teaching Kids about Boundaries," Child Mind Institute, accessed September 14, 2022, https://childmind.org/article/teaching-kids-boundaries-empathy/.

18. Katherine Lee, "How to Set Healthy Boundaries for Kids," VeryWellFamily, April 1, 2021, https://www.verywellfamily.com/whos-the-boss-how-to-set-healthy-boundaries-for-kids-3956403.

19. Jason Rafferty, "Gender Identity Development in Children," Healthy Children, accessed September 14, 2022, https://www.healthychildren.org/English/ages-stages/gradeschool/Pages/Gender-Identity-and-Gender-Confusion-In-Children.aspx.

20. Rebecca Fraser-Thrill, "Major Domains in Child Development," VeryWellFamily, November 27, 2021, https://www.verywellfamily.com/definition-of-domain-3288323#toc-cognitive-development.

21. New York University, "Young Children's Sense of Self."

22. American Academy of Pediatrics, "Healthy Communication with Your Child," Cradle thru College Care, accessed September 14, 2022, https://www.cradlethrucollege.com/Healthy-Communication-With-Your-Child.

23. Amy Morin, "5 Major Problems with Helicopter Parenting," *Psychology Today*, February 19, 2018, https://www.psychologytoday.com/us/blog/what-mentally-strong-people-dont-do/201802/5-major-problems-helicopter-parenting.

24. Kaitlin Luna, "Helicopter Parenting May Negatively Affect Children's Emotional Well-Being, Behavior," American Psychological Association, June 18, 2018, https://www .apa.org/news/press/releases/2018/06/helicopter-parenting.

25. Joel L. Young, "The Effects of Helicopter Parenting," *Psychology Today*, January 25, 2017, https://www.psychologytoday.com/us/blog/when-your-adult-child-breaks-your -heart/201701/the-effects-helicopter-parenting.

26. Leon F. Seltzer, "From Parent-Pleasing to People-Pleasing (Part 2 of 3)," *Psychology Today*, July 25, 2008, https://www.psychologytoday.com/us/blog/evolution-the -self/200807/parent-pleasing-people-pleasing-part-2-3.

27. Carrie Barron, "Hands-Off Parenting for Resilient, Resourceful Children," *Psychology Today*, April 28, 2016, https://www.psychologytoday.com/us/blog/the-creativity -cure/201604/hands-parenting-resilient-resourceful-children.

Chapter 17 Identity Issues and the Neurocycle

1. Krischa Esquivel et al., "3.2: How Children Develop Identity," *The Role of Equity and Diversity in Early Childhood Education*, January 4, 2021, https://socialsci.libretexts.org /Bookshelves/Early_Childhood_Education/Book:_The_Role_of_Equity_and_Diversity_in _Early_Childhood_Education_(Esquivel_Elam_Paris_and_Tafoya).

2. D. Pepler and K. Bierman, "With a Little Help from My Friends: The Importance of Peer Relationships for Social-Emotional Development," Robert Wood Johnson Foundation, November 1, 2018, https://www.rwjf.org/en/library/research/2018/11/with-a-little -help-from-my-friends--the-importance-of-peer-relationships-for-social-emotional-de velopment.html.

Chapter 18 Social Interactions

1. Richard Armitage, "Bullying in Children: Impact on Child Health," *BMJ Paediatrics Open* 5, no. 1 (2021), https://doi.org/10.1136%2Fbmjpo-2020-000939.

2. Gokmen Arslan, Kelly-Ann Allen, and Ahmet Tanhan, "School Bullying, Mental Health, and Wellbeing in Adolescents: Mediating Impact of Positive Psychological Orientations," *Child Indicators Research* 14 (2021): 1007–26, https://link.springer.com/article /10.1007/s12187-020-09780-2.

3. Francesc Sidera, Elisabet Serrat, and Carles Rostan, "Effects of Cybervictimization on the Mental Health of Primary School Students," *Frontiers in Public Health* (May 24, 2021), https://doi.org/10.3389/fpubh.2021.588209.

4. Gokmen Arslan, Kelly-Ann Allen, and Ahmet Tanhan, "School Bullying, Mental Health, and Wellbeing in Adolescents: Mediating Impact of Positive Psychological Orientations," *Child Indicators Research* 14 (2021), https://link.springer.com/article/10.1007 /s12187-020-09780-2.

5. Sidera, Serrat, and Rostan, "Effects of Cybervictimization."

6. Gary Drevitch, "How Children Develop Empathy," *Psychology Today*, May 19, 2019, https://www.psychologytoday.com/us/blog/smart-parenting-smarter-kids/201905/how -children-develop-empathy.

7. Ugo Uche, "Empathy Promotes Emotional Resiliency," *Psychology Today*, May 18, 2010, https://www.psychologytoday.com/us/blog/promoting-empathy-your-teen/201005 /empathy-promotes-emotional-resiliency.

8. Laura Howard, "Why Is Empathy Important for Kids? Tips to Build Empathy in Children," Atlanta Innovative Counseling Center, April 29, 2020, https://www.atlantainno vativecounseling.com/aicc-blog/why-is-empathy-important-for-kids-tips-to-build-empathy -in-children.

9. Kathy Reschke, "Who Am I? Developing a Sense of Self and Belonging," Zero to Three, April 10, 2020, https://www.zerotothree.org/resources/2648-who-am-i-developing -a-sense-of-self-and-belonging.

10. Ross Thompson and Emily Newton, "Baby Altruists? Examining the Complexity of Prosocial Motivation in Young Children," *Infancy* 18, no. 1 (2012): 120–33, https:// onlinelibrary.wiley.com/doi/abs/10.1111/j.1532-7078.2012.00139.x.

11. Fatima Malik and Raman Marwaha, "Developmental Stages of Social Emotional Development in Children," *StatPearls*, May 10, 2022, https://www.ncbi.nlm.nih.gov/books /NBK534819/.

12. Ioana Lepadatu, "How Children See Their Parents: A Short Intergeneration Comparative Analysis," *Procedia: Social and Behavioral Sciences* 187 (2015): 5–9, https://www.science direct.com/science/article/pii/S1877042815017954/pdf?md5=ee7f31c5aafff4f4580380d53e4 0e034&pid=1-s2.0-S1877042815017954-main.pdf&_valck=1.

13. National Society for the Prevention of Cruelty to Children, "Attachment and Child Development," NSPCC Learning, August 10, 2021, https://learning.nspcc.org.uk/child -health-development/attachment-early-years#heading-top.

14. National Society for the Prevention of Cruelty to Children, "Attachment and Child Development."

15. Anna Freud National Centre for Children and Families, "Attachment and Child Development," Mentally Healthy Schools, accessed September 22, 2022, https://www.men tallyhealthyschools.org.uk/mental-health-needs/attachment-and-child-development/.

16. Madeline Harms et al., "Instrumental and Cognitive Flexibility Processes Are Impaired in Children Exposed to Early Life Stress," *Developmental Science* 21, no. 4 (October 19, 2017), https://doi.org/10.1111/desc.12596.

Chapter 20 Labels

1. National Institute of Mental Health, "Attention-Deficit/Hyperactivity Disorder," U.S. Department of Health and Human Services, accessed September 14, 2022, https://www .nimh.nih.gov/health/statistics/attention-deficit-hyperactivity-disorder-adhd.

2. Christel Renoux et al., "Prescribing Trends of Attention-Deficit Hyperactivity Disorder (ADHD) Medications in UK Primary Care, 1995–2015," *British Journal of Clinical Pharmacology* 82, no. 3 (May 4, 2016): 858–68, https://doi.org/10.1111%2Fbcp.13000.

3. Jane Costello, William Copeland, and Adrian Angold, "The Great Smoky Mountains Study: Developmental Epidemiology in the Southeastern United States," *Social Psychiatry and Psychiatric Epidemiology* 51, no. 5 (March 24, 2016): 639–46, https://doi.org/10.1007 %2Fs00127-015-1168-1.

4. Allen J. Frances, "Keith Connors, Father of ADHD, Regrets Its Current Misuse," *Psychology Today*, March 28, 2016, https://www.psychologytoday.com/intl/blog/saving -normal/201603/keith-connors-father-adhd-regrets-its-current-misuse.

5. Jimena Tavel, "ADHD Meds Don't Lead to Higher Grades or More Learning, FIU Study Finds," *Miami Herald*, May 24, 2022, https://www.miamiherald.com/news/local /education/article261714172.html.

6. Yunhye Oh, Yoo-Sook Joung, and Jinseob Kim, "Association between Attention Deficit Hyperactivity Disorder Medication and Depression: A 10-Year Follow-Up Self-Controlled Case Study," *Clinical Psychopharmacology and Neuroscience* 20, no. 2 (2022): 320–29, https://www.cpn.or.kr/journal/view.html?volume=20&number=2&spage=320#B19.

7. Peter C. Gøtzsche, "A Hopelessly Flawed Seminar in 'The Lancet' about Suicide," *Mad in America*, June 1, 2022, https://www.madinamerica.com/2022/06/flawed-lancet-suicide/.

8. Sami Timimi, *Insane Medicine: How the Mental Health Industry Creates Damaging Treatment Traps and How You Can Escape Them* (self-published, 2021).

9. Peter Simons, "Researchers Question the 'Adequacy and Legitimacy' of ADHD Diagnosis," *Mad in America*, September 5, 2017, https://www.madinamerica.com/2017/09/researchers-question-adequacy-legitimacy-adhd-diagnosis/.

10. Caroline Leaf, "Mind-Mapping: A Therapeutic Technique for Closed-Head Injury" (master's thesis, University of Pretoria, 1990). See also Caroline Leaf, "The Mind-Mapping Approach: A Model and Framework for Geodesic Learning" (DPhil diss., University of Pretoria, 1997).

11. Caroline Leaf, "Switch on Your Brain 5-Step Learning Process: Classroom Results," Dr.Leaf.com, 2013, https://cdn.shopify.com/s/files/1/1810/9163/files/Web-page-AA-research-project.pdf?134.

12. Corinne Rees, "Childhood Attachment," *British Journal of General Practice* 57, no. 544 (2007): 920–22, https://www.ncbi.nlm.nih.gov/pmc/articles/PMC2169321/.

13. Gøtzsche, "A Hopelessly Flawed Seminar."

14. Paula Caplan, "Psychiatry's Bible, the DSM, Is Doing More Harm Than Good," *Washington Post*, April 27, 2012, https://www.washingtonpost.com/opinions/psychiatrys-bible-the-dsm-is-doing-more-harm-than-good/2012/04/27/gIQAqyoWlT_story.html. See also Paula J. Caplan, "How Do They Decide Who Is Normal? The Bizarre, but True, Tale of the *DSM* Process," *Canadian Psychology / Psychologie Canadienne* 32, no. 2 (1991): 162–70.

15. Juho Honkasilta, "Voices behind and beyond the Label: The Master Narrative of ADHD (De)constructed by Diagnosed Children and Their Parents," *Jyväskylä Studies in Education, Psychology and Social Research* 553 (2016), https://jyx.jyu.fi/handle/123456789/49720.

16. Julie Allan, "Problem Behaviour in Children Is Not Always a Mental Disorder," *The Conversation*, June 11, 2014, https://theconversation.com/problem-behaviour-in-children-is-not-always-a-mental-disorder-22379.

17. Martin Whitely et al., "Influence of Birth Month on the Probability of Western Australian Children Being Treated for ADHD," *The Medical Journal of Australia* 206, no. 2 (February 6, 2017): 85, https://www.mja.com.au/journal/2017/206/2/influence-birth-month-probability-western-australian-children-being-treated-adhd.

18. Timimi, *Insane Medicine.*

19. Allen Frances, "The Epidemic of Attention Deficit Disorder: Real or Fad?," *Psychiatric Times*, May 19, 2011, https://www.psychiatrictimes.com/view/epidemic-attention-deficit-disorder-real-or-fad.

20. Peter Simons, "*Lancet Psychiatry*'s Controversial ADHD Study: Errors, Criticism, and Response," *Mad in America*, May 15, 2017, https://www.madinamerica.com/2017/05/lancet-psychiatrys-controversial-adhd-study-errors-criticism-responses/.

21. Benedict Carey, "Keith Conners, Psychologist Who Set Standard for Diagnosing A.D.H.D., Dies at 84," *New York Times*, July 13, 2017, https://www.nytimes.com/2017/07/13/health/keith-conners-dead-psychologist-adhd-diagnosing.html.

22. Frances, "Keith Connors."

23. Eric Maisel, "Sami Timimi on ADHD, Autism and Children's Mental Health," *Psychology Today*, April 1, 2016, https://www.psychologytoday.com/us/blog/rethinking-mental-health/201604/sami-timimi-adhd-autism-and-childrens-mental-health.

24. Maisel, "Sami Timimi."

25. Sami Timimi, *Naughty Boys: Anti-Social Behaviour, ADHD and the Role of Culture* (New York: Red Globe Press, 2005); Sami Timimi, Neil Gardner, and Brian McCabe, *The Myth of Autism: Medicalising Men's and Boys' Social and Emotional Competence* (New York: Red Globe Press, 2010); Timimi, *Insane Medicine.*

26. Sami Timimi, *A Straight Talking Introduction to Children's Mental Health Problems* (Wyastone Leys, UK: PCCS Books, 2013), 129–31.

Chapter 21 Labels and the Neurocycle

1. Amanda Penn, "Positive Labels: Why They're Actually Hurting Your Kids," Shortform, January 11, 2020, https://www.shortform.com/blog/positive-labels/.

2. Raunak Pillai, Carrie Sherry, and Lisa Fazio, "How Repetition Affects What Kids and Adults Believe," *Frontiers for Young Minds*, April 9, 2021, https://kids.frontiersin.org /articles/10.3389/frym.2021.582203.

Chapter 22 Sleep Issues

1. Yankun Sun et al., "The Bidirectional Relationship between Sleep Duration and Depression in Community-Dwelling Middle-Aged and Elderly Individuals: Evidence from a Longitudinal Study," *Sleep Medicine* 52 (December 2018): 221–29, https://linkinghub.elsevier .com/retrieve/pii/S1389945718300856.

2. Rob Newsom, "Trauma and Sleep," Sleep Foundation, April 29, 2022, https://www .sleepfoundation.org/mental-health/trauma-and-sleep.

3. Amy Licis, "Sleep Disorders: Assessment and Treatment in Preschool-Aged Children," *Child and Adolescent Psychiatry Clinics of North America* 26, no. 3 (July 2017): 587–95, https://pubmed.ncbi.nlm.nih.gov/28577611/.

4. Kevin Carter et al., "Common Sleep Disorders in Children," *American Family Physician* 89, no. 5 (2014): 368–77, https://www.aafp.org/afp/2014/0301/p368.html.

5. "Pediatric Obstructive Sleep Apnea," Mayo Clinic, accessed September 15, 2022, https://www.mayoclinic.org/diseases-conditions/pediatric-sleep-apnea/symptoms-causes /syc-20376196.

6. "Sleep Terrors and Sleepwalking," Nationwide Children's Hospital, accessed September 15, 2022, https://www.nationwidechildrens.org/conditions/sleep-terrors-and-sleep walking.

7. "Nightmares and Night Terrors," Stanford Medicine Children's Health, accessed September 15, 2022, https://www.stanfordchildrens.org/en/topic/default?id=nightmares -and-night-terrors-90-P02257.

8. Alexa Fry, "How Blue Light Affects Kids' Sleep," Sleep Foundation, April 18, 2022, https://www.sleepfoundation.org/children-and-sleep/how-blue-light-affects-kids-sleep.

9. Julia Rodriguez, "Does Pre-Bed Video Gaming Ruin Your Sleep?," Advanced Sleep Medicine Services, accessed September 15, 2022, https://www.sleepdr.com/the-sleep-blog /does-pre-bed-video-gaming-ruin-your-sleep/.

10. Christopher Curley, "Only Half of U.S. Children Get Enough Sleep: Why That's a Serious Problem," Healthline, October 24, 2019, https://www.healthline.com/health-news /children-lack-of-sleep-health-problems.

11. "Sleeplessness," *British Medical Journal* 2, no. 1761 (1894): 719, http://www.jstor.org /stable/20229974.

12. Danielle Pacheco and Nilong Vyas, "Children and Sleep," Sleep Foundation, March 11, 2022, https://www.sleepfoundation.org/children-and-sleep; Harvard Medical School, "Changes in Sleep with Age," Healthy Sleep, accessed September 15, 2022, http:// healthysleep.med.harvard.edu/healthy/science/variations/changes-in-sleep-with-age.

13. Matthew J. Wolf-Meyer, "Myths of Modern American Sleep: Naturalizing Primordial Sleep, Blaming Technological Distractions, and Pathologizing Children," *Science as Culture* 24, no. 2 (August 19, 2014): 205–26, http://dx.doi.org/10.1080/09505431.2014.94 5411.

14. Lisa Anne Matricciani et al., "Never Enough Sleep: A Brief History of Sleep Recommendations for Children," *Pediatrics* 129, no. 3 (2012): 548–56, https://publications.aap .org/pediatrics/article-abstract/129/3/548/31684/Never-Enough-Sleep-A-Brief-History-of -Sleep?redirectedFrom=fulltext.

15. Anjolii Diaz et al., "Children's Sleep and Academic Achievement: The Moderating Role of Effortful Control," *International Journal of Behavioral Development* 41, no. 2 (March 2017): 275–84, https://www.ncbi.nlm.nih.gov/pmc/articles/PMC5327793/.

16. Julie C. Lumeng, "Future Directions for Research on Sleep Durations in Pediatric Populations," *Sleep* 33, no. 10 (October 2010): 1281–82, https://academic.oup.com/sleep /article/33/10/1281/2454437?login=true; Doris Erwin, "An Analytical Study of Children's Sleep," *The Pedagogical Seminary and Journal of Genetic Psychology* 45, no. 1 (September 11, 2012): 199–226, https://www.tandfonline.com/doi/abs/10.1080/08856559.1934.10534255.

17. Tim Olds et al., "The Relationship between Sex, Age, Geography, and Time in Bed in Adolescents: A Meta-Analysis of Data from 23 Countries," *Sleep Medicine Reviews* 14, no. 6 (December 2010): 371–78, https://doi.org/10.1016/j.smrv.2009.12.002.

18. University of Copenhagen, "Stress Transmitter Wakes Your Brain More Than 100 Times a Night—and It Is Perfectly Normal," ScienceDaily, July 14, 2022, https://www .sciencedaily.com/releases/2022/07/220714103016.htm.

19. Scott Kinlein et al., "Dysregulated Hypothalamic-Pituitary-Adrenal Axis Function Contributes to Altered Endocrine and Neurobehavioral Responses to Acute Stress," *Frontiers in Psychology* 6, no. 31 (March 13, 2015), https://www.frontiersin.org/articles/10 .3389/fpsyt.2015.00031/full.

20. Michael J. Breus, "The Effects of Cortisol on Your Sleep," *Psychology Today*, April 10, 2020, https://www.psychologytoday.com/us/blog/sleep-newzzz/202004/the-effects -cortisol-your-sleep.

21. Sarah Khan and Rafeeq Alam Khan, "Chronic Stress Leads to Anxiety and Depression," *Annals of Psychiatry and Mental Health* 5, no. 1 (January 27, 2017): 1091, https://www .jscimedcentral.com/Psychiatry/psychiatry-5-1091.pdf.

22. Pacheco and Vyas, "Children and Sleep."

23. "Size of the Sleep Economy Worldwide from 2019 to 2024," Statista, July 27, 2022, https://www.statista.com/statistics/1119471/size-of-the-sleep-economy-worldwide/.

24. Valérie Simard et al., "Longitudinal Study of Bad Dreams in Preschool-Aged Children: Prevalence, Demographic Correlates, Risk, and Protective Factors," *Sleep* 31, no. 1 (January 1, 2008): 62–70, https://www.ncbi.nlm.nih.gov/pmc/articles/PMC2225564/.

25. Eric Suni and Alex Dimitriu, "Dreams," Sleep Foundation, March 18, 2022, https:// www.sleepfoundation.org/dreams.

26. "Nightmares in Children," Cleveland Clinic, accessed September 15, 2022, https:// my.clevelandclinic.org/health/articles/14297-nightmares-in-children.

27. Tore Nielsen, "The Twenty-Four-Hour Mind: The Role of Sleep and Dreaming in Our Emotional Lives (Review)," *Sleep* 34, no. 4 (April 1, 2011): 549–50, https://www.ncbi .nlm.nih.gov/pmc/articles/PMC3065266/.

28. University of Adelaide, "Want to Control Your Dreams? Here's How You Can," ScienceDaily, October 19, 2017, https://www.sciencedaily.com/releases/2017/10/171019100812 .htm.

Chapter 23 Sleep Issues and the Neurocycle

1. "A Healthy Night's Sleep Starts the Moment You Wake Up," National Sleep Foundation, March 13, 2022, https://www.thensf.org/a-healthy-nights-sleep-starts-the-moment -you-wake-up/.

2. Eleesha Lockett, "Why Do We Have Recurring Nightmares?," Healthline, January 28, 2019, https://www.healthline.com/health/healthy-sleep/recurring-nightmares.

Dr. Caroline Leaf is a communication pathologist and clinical neuroscientist specializing in psychoneurobiology. Her passion is to help people see the power of the mind to change the brain, control chaotic thinking, and find mental peace. She is the author of the bestselling books *Cleaning Up Your Mental Mess, Switch On Your Brain, Think and Eat Yourself Smart, The Perfect You, Think, Learn, Succeed,* and many more. She is also the author of the top-rated podcast *Cleaning Up the Mental Mess,* which has over forty million downloads. She currently does extensive research and teaches at various academic, medical, corporate, and neuroscience conferences, as well as in religious and spiritual institutions around the world. Dr. Leaf and her husband, Mac, have four adult children and live between Dallas and Miami.

5 Simple Steps. Less Stress.
More Happiness.

Backed by clinical research and illustrated with compelling case studies, Dr. Caroline Leaf's latest book provides a scientifically proven five-step plan, the Neurocycle, to find and eliminate the root of anxiety, depression, and intrusive thoughts in your life so you can experience dramatically improved mental and physical health.

MORE RESOURCES FOR A
HEALTHY BRAIN

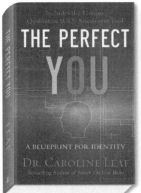

Connect with
CAROLINE

VISIT
DrLeaf.com

to learn more about Dr. Leaf and her
research, read her blog, listen to her podcast,
and follow her speaking schedule!

Also follow her on social media.

drleaf

DrCarolineLeaf

drcarolineleaf

Dr. Caroline Leaf

CLEANING UP THE MENTAL MESS

WITH DR. CAROLINE LEAF

SIMPLE & SCIENTIFIC
STRATEGIES TO HELP YOU
TAKE BACK CONTROL OF YOUR
MENTAL HEALTH & LIFE

AVAILABLE WHEREVER YOU LISTEN TO PODCASTS

ANCHOR.FM/CLEANINGUPTHEMENTALMESS

THE ONLY SCIENTIFICALLY TESTED DAILY BRAIN DETOX PROGRAM

neurocycle
DR. CAROLINE LEAF

• featured in •

Manage stress, anxiety, depression, and intrusive thoughts with the **first ever brain detox app!**

Learn more at **neurocycle.app** or download on the **App Store or Google Play.**

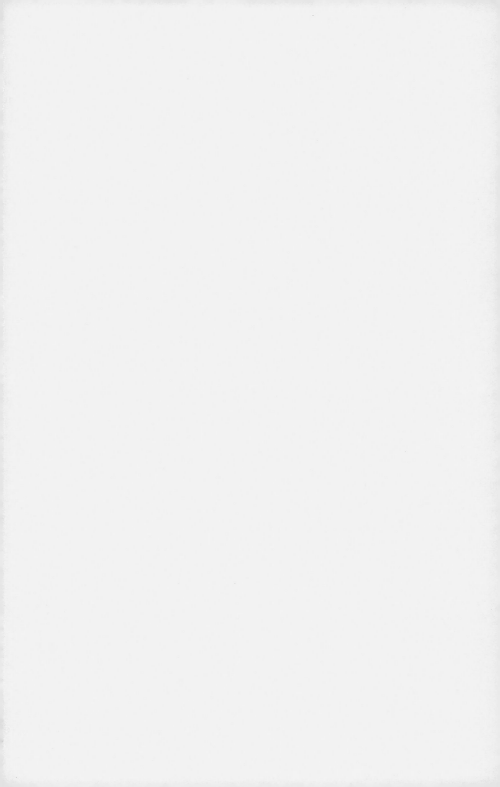